Search Your Middle Eastern & European Genealogy

Search Your Middle Eastern & European Genealogy

◆

In the Former Ottoman Empire's Records and Online

Anne Hart

ASJA Press
New York Lincoln Shanghai

Search Your Middle Eastern & European Genealogy
In the Former Ottoman Empire's Records and Online

ASJA Press
an imprint of iUniverse, Inc.

For information address:
iUniverse, Inc.
2021 Pine Lake Road, Suite 100
Lincoln, NE 68512
www.iuniverse.com

ISBN: 0-595-31811-8

Printed in the United States of America

Contents

Introduction

Have any of your ancestors ever lived under the former Ottoman Empire? The Ottoman Empire lasted from 1300 until 1922. In 1924 Kemal Ataturk abolished the Muslim caliphate and founded the Republic of Turkey. So regardless of the language spoken by your ancestors—Slavic, Arabic, Greek, Judezmo, Uralic, Yiddish, Romanian, or Turkish, the Ottoman Empire controlled and kept careful census records in Turkish using Arabic script in the following countries of Europe and the Middle East known today, but not necessarily before 1924 as the following names:

Hungary, Yugoslavia, Croatia, Bosnia, Albania, Macedonia, Greece, Romania, Moldova, Bulgaria, southern Ukraine, Turkey, Georgia, Armenia, Iraq, Kuwait, Cyprus, Syria, Lebanon, Israel/Palestine, Jordan, Eastern and Western Saudi Arabia, Oman, Bahrain, eastern Yemen, Egypt, northern Libya, Tunisia, and northern Algeria.

In addition, more recent records in Arabic or in the language of the country emphasized are kept in the national archives and in the courts dealing with property-related issues, assets left behind, divorce decrees, and other legal documents. Often when a population is forced out, the individual country, such as present-day Egypt, may then determine that assets, property, and religious items taken away or left behind such as Judaica, Hellenica, and Armenica are declared antiquities of that country that cannot be removed.

You can approach genealogy by running a teen genealogy camp for foreign travel. If you get enough tourists, you can go free and emphasize genealogy research. Another approach is to collect memorabilia from your ethnic group such as Hellenica, Judaica, Armenica, Arabica, and other objects. Every object you collect in genealogy as far as records or actual objects opens a door. As you step over the threshold, you can see time and place in the context of that culture.

1

Key: Seven Steps to Begin

Key: Find out in which **local district or '*kaza*'** your ancestor lived. Ottomans called their annual census the *sicil-i nüfus* after 1881 or the *nüfus* between 1831-1850. You can research the **Ottoman Census and Population Registers** named in Turkish the **Nüfus Defter**.

Genealogy opens portals to the artistic, cultural, religious, social, historical, and economic environment in which a particular item was designed and brought forth, from people to their icons. Genealogy is cultural geography as well as a history and ethnography of human genes.

Look at ethnic objects along with the census or other genealogy records. There are so many locations to cover the settlement of your peoples, the human race. Genealogy allows you to view a juxtaposition of demography with memorabilia and ethnic or religious items. Learn how to research your own group and show others about the life of the people you choose to study, their history and design.

That's why running a teen (or other age group) genealogy camp is fun, especially in researching the former Ottoman Empire—or any other location that you want to emphasize, perhaps your own ethnic history. How do you start?

The Family History Library (Salt Lake City, UT) has a catalog that can give you rewarding and rich research ideas. So if it's the former Ottoman Empire you want to emphasize, or how the world of antiquity blends into your relatively modern genealogy, first check the Family History Library catalog (Salt Lake City, UT) for books, microfilms, civil registration, localities and jurisdictions.

Then search the Ottoman Census and Population Registers by country named in Turkish the Nüfus Defter. Check the online library catalog at Bogaziçi University (a.k.a. the University of the Bosphorus). See http://www.geog.port.ac.uk/hist-bound/country rep/ottoman.htm. Also check out the flyer: http://www.hanover.edu/haq center/Bogazici-Flyer.html

Records are found in the Ottoman Census archives in Turkey pertaining to tax collection during the Ottoman rule. Moslems weren't taxed. Before 1881, each census focused on tabulating male names to find Moslem men to conscript into the military service and non-Moslem men to pay personal tax. Search

1

records according to the religion and ethnic group. Start your search with the list of countries under the Ottomans and pick your ancestor's homeland.

Egypt was under the former Ottoman Empire. Therefore, if you are a Jew from Egypt (regardless of whether your family members are Ashkenazim, Sepharadim, or Mizrahi), check out **The Historical Society Of Jews From Egypt**. Their Web site is at: http://hsje.org/. This site is designed to gather, and provide historical and current information on the Jews From Egypt, one of the most ancient established societies in the world."

According to their Web site, "We will attempt to cover the period from Joseph Saadia el Fayoumi (Saadia Gaon) to the present day." The Web site notes that, "This organization shall be known as Historical Society of Jews from Egypt, and not of Egypt or of Egyptian Jews, but from Egypt for the purpose will be to include all our co-religionists whose lineage have sojourned in the Jewish Communities of Egypt."

Contact them if you had relatives who lived in the Jewish communities of Egypt. Some Romanian and Greek Jews also lived in the Jewish communities of Egypt and some Ashkenazim also. According to their Web site, "The aims of this society are to preserve, maintain, coordinate the implementation, and to convey our rich heritage to our children and grand children's, using all educational means at our disposal to bring into being the necessary foundations."

Referring to Romania and in particular, Bessarabia, some Romanian Jews migrated to Palestine in the Ottoman era. This migration included Ashkenazim and Sephardim. Numerous Sephardim and Mizrahi had migrated to Palestine in earlier times and a smaller number of Ashkenazim. Your genealogy source here could be to consult a Jewish genealogy journal such as Avotaynu at: http://www.avotaynu.com.

According to the Jews of Egypt Web site at: http://www.us-israel.org/jsource/anti-semitism/egjews.html, "In 1979, the Egyptian Jewish community became the first in the Arab world to establish official contact with Israel. Israel now has an embassy in Cairo and a consulate general in Alexandria. At present, the few remaining Jews are free to practice Judaism without any restrictions or harassment. Shaar Hashamayim is the only functioning synagogue in Cairo. Of the many synagogues in Alexandria only the Eliahu Hanabi is open for worship.[4]" The source of this information on their Web site is listed as Jewish Communities of the World.

According to researcher, Kahlile Mehr, "For searching the Ottoman period in most countries under the former Ottoman Empire, the researcher would have to read Turkish in Arabic script. The Family History library was able to film some

Christian church records in Israel during the 1980s. But for most of the populace, the commonly known genealogical sources of the West simply do not exist. The best known source is the Nufus registers.

"The Family History Library filmed the Nufus registers in the Israeli State Archives for Israel, parts of Jordan and Egypt. A description of these can be found in the catalog at www.familysearch.org.

"If you're searching various ethnic groups in Bessarabia, it was not part of Romania except during the period between World War I and II. It was historically part of the Ottoman and then the Russian Empire. Today, it is Moldova."

There was a time in the late 18th century and early 19th century when Bessarabia fell out of the Ottoman Empire and became under the rule of the Russians. At that time a large immigration of German Christians and German Jews as well as Jews from Poland, Ukraine, Belarus, and surrounding areas flocked to Bessarabia. So you have a community of Protestant Germans in Bessarabia along with German and Polish Jews. The immigration took place as soon as Bessarabia fell into Russian hands and out of Ottoman hands for that period of time.

You can trace names that show up in Poland such as Herkowicz to Romanian, where the spelling changes to Herkowitz and later to the Romanian spelling, Herkovici, in some cases. Countries change names. Bessarabia, once a place with its own name rather than a province in a country, then becomes an area within a country, and finally today, falling in the borders of Moldova and Romania.

Step 1: Translating Names

Don't skip generations. Each generation is a vital link in countries where thousands have the same name. Check out the Middle EastGenWeb Project at: http://www.rootsweb.com/~mdeastgw/index.html.

Some religious names are used by Moslems and Christians. Christian European names are translated into Arabic in Arabic-speaking countries. For example, in Lebanon, Peter becomes Boutros and George becomes Girgis or Abdul Messikh, meaning servant of the Messiah (Christ). Shammout (strong), Deeb (wolf), or Dib (bear). Nissim (miracles) is used by Jewish Levantines, and Adam is used by Jewish, Christian, and Moslem families.

Women had the choice of taking their husband's surnames or keeping their maiden names. Neutral names, used by Moslems, Jews, and Christians such as Ibrahim (Abraham) or Yusef (Joseph) came from the Old Testament. In Lebanon, Christians often used neutral names such as Tewfik (fortunate).

Arabic-speaking and Turkic-speaking countries didn't use surnames until after the end of the Ottoman Empire. Then in Lebanon and Syria many Christians took as their surnames European or Biblical first male names such as the Arabic versions of George, Jacob, Thomas, and Peter which were in Arabic: Girgis, Yacoub, Toumas, and Boutros. Others took popular surnames describing their occupations such as Haddad meaning 'smith.'

After 1928 in Turkey, but not in any of the other Middle Eastern nations, a modified Latin alphabet replaced Arabic script. Four years later (1932) the Turkish Linguistic Society simplified the language to unify the people. Surnames were required in 1934 and, old titles indicating professions and classes were dropped. (See "Turkey" Web site at: http://www.kusadasitravel.com/turkey.html.)

In Middle Eastern countries under the former Ottoman Empire, such as Lebanon/Syria, each child was given a first name but most people in the Middle East had no surname until 1932. Also the father's given name was given as a middle name such as Yusef Girgis, meaning Yusef (Joseph), son of George. It came in handy in the days before surnames were required. Now it's used as a middle name.

Many Syrian and Lebanese families, particularly Christians, after 1932 took similar names such as Peter Jacobs or George Thomas. The name 'Thomas' in Lebanon is spelled in translation as either Touma or Toumas. Many Assyrian males in Northern Iraq took the popular name Sargon, an ancient king.

When surnames in Lebanon became a requirement, you have very popular names such as Peter George Khoury in America being Boutros Girgis Khouri in Lebanon or Syria when translated into Arabic. In the Levant, daughters have a first name and their father's given name meaning "daughter of Yusef" or Ayah Yusef. Translated into English at Ellis Island, it could have become Aya Joseph.

When surnames became a requirement, many included professions or place names, especially Halaby (from Aleppo) or Antaky (from Antioch). The largest Lebanese community in America is in Dearborn, Michigan.

In Lebanon, most names were Christian prior to 1870, and the Christian names could also be European, especially Greek names like Petros (Peter) which later becomes Boutros in Arabic. If you're searching Assyrians, check out the Assyrian Nation Communities Web site at: http://www.assyriannation.com/communities/index.php.

Researching Assyrian Genealogy
Assyrian Presbyterian Genealogy Records Research:

According to the Public Services and Outreach division of the Presbyterian Historical Society, while the Presbyterian Church sent missionaries to the Middle East, materials at the Presbyterian Historical Society document their activities there and do not contain any information about individuals from the Middle East who immigrated to the United States. To get an idea of the types of materials at the Presbyterian Historical Society useful for genealogists, review the following sections of their website at:http://www.history.pcusa.org/famhist/ or http://www.history.pcusa.org/collect/. This second page also provides links to their on-line finding aids, http://www.history.pcusa.org/finding/index.html, and catalog, CALVIN, http://www.history.pcusa.org/dbtw-wpd/WebOPACmenu.htm. Search each to see what they might have for your area of interest.

Records of individual congregations are the main resource for family history research at the society. There are no centralized denominational registers of church memberships, baptisms, or marriages; nor is there a comprehensive index to the thousands of family names included in the records in our holdings.

To start a search, it is essential to know both the location (city and state) and the full and correct name of the congregation associated with the individual you are researching. They do not have lists of churches by township, city, or county, or street name cross indexes.

Research genealogy records of members of the Assyrian Presbyterian Church in the US or in Iraq and Iran. Search Assyrian colonies in various US cities for genealogy records related to the Presbyterian Church.

If you are searching Assyrian records, and your family belonged to the Presbyterian Church, check out the Presbyterian Church Historical Society at: http://history.pcusa.org/finding/phs%20379.xml#scopecontent where you can find book titles and/or records such as the Assyrian and National Church History, volumes 1 and 2. Look up Isaac BMoorhatch (1880–) Papers, 1938, Finding Aid to Record Group 379, © Presbyterian Historical Society , Philadelphia, PA 19147.

From the early 20th century, many Assyrians immigrating to the US joined the Presbyterian church. This is due to the missionaries in Persia and Iraq in the early 20th century. For example, In 1910 Isaac Moorhatch established the Assyrian Presbyterian Church of Gary, Indiana. In 1923 he arrived in Philadelphia, where the Assyrian colony asked him to serve as their pastor. After ordination, he took charge of the Persian/Assyrian Presbyterian Mission. He served this mission until retirement in 1950.

So your first step is to find out where the Assyrian colonies were in the US. Was one of your relatives a missionary in a country then under the former Ottoman Empire?

Isaac Moorhatch was born in Urumia, Persia, the son of Presbyterian missionaries. He grew up in Iran and attended the Presbyterian college in Urumia. In 1897 he began working as an evangelical and educational missionary for the Board of Foreign Missions (PCUSA).

So search the Presbyterian colleges in various Middle Eastern countries when they were under the Ottoman Empire. In 1909 Moorhatch arrived in the United States with the intention of entering a Presbyterian seminary and returning to work among the Persian Moslems after graduation. In the end he enrolled in the Baptist Theological Seminary in Kansas City, KS in 1912.

According to the Web site of the Presbyterian Church History records at: http://history.pcusa.org/finding/phs%20379.xml#scopecontent, "In 1910 Moorhatch established the Assyrian Presbyterian Church of Gary, IN. In 1923 he arrived in Philadelphia, where the Assyrian colony asked him to serve as their pastor. After ordination, he took charge of the Persian/Assyrian Presbyterian Mission. He served this mission until retirement in 1950."

If you research the collection of Presbyterian Church History records, you can read Moorhatch's two-volume manuscript work titled: ***Assyrian and National Church History: History of Iran: Rise of Islam.*** The work is written in Aramaic. Each volume includes a table of contents. So if you come from an Assyrian family or any other ethnic group that is able to read Aramaic, such as numerous Jews and a few groups in Syria, you can read or even translate the Aramaic to English.

If you're searching the collection of Presbyterian Church history, records less than 50 years old are restricted. Contact the archivist. The collection was processed in 1993. Your reference point would be: *Finding Aid to Record Group 379, Box 1 Folder 1. Assyrian and National Church History, volumes 1 and 2. Folder 2–3.*

After 1870, in Lebanon and Syria names in Christian families became Arabic rather than European due to increasing pressure by the Ottoman Empire on Christians to use Arabic instead of Greek names. After the demise of the Ottoman Empire at the close of World War I, Hellenistic names such as Kostaki (Constantine) became popular in Beirut.

The distinctly Christian Lebanese surnames Khoury (priest) or Kourban sprang up again when Lebanon became a French protectorate. Neutral, Greek, and Old Testament names also return. You see many French first names in Christian families between 1914 and 1950.

After the 1950s, Christian and French first names dwindle, and Arabic names appear. If your ancestors were Moslem, instead of a surname prior to 1932, you were known as "son of" (Ibn) as in Ibn Omar, for a male, and for a married woman with children called, "mother of" (om) as in Om Kolthum, (mother of Kolthum).

You'd be called mother of your first born son, (Om___Name of first born son) (Om Ahmed). If you had no sons, you'd be called mother of your first born daughter (Om Rania) (Om___Name of first born daughter). Single women often were called "daughter of" as in Bint Ahmed (daughter of Ahmed).

Arabic women's first names were plentiful, popular, and used at mainly at home. Examples include Samara, Zobaida, Rayana, Rania, Anissa, Dayala, Azma, Aya, or Salwa. Children had first names.

If your ancestors were Armenian living in the Levant you might have the name Ter or Der before a surname designating descent from an Armenian Apostolic priest followed by a name ending in ian or yan meaning "son of" such as Manvelian or a place name such as Halebian (from Aleppo) when translated into English. If you're Armenian searching Turkish census records, the pre-1920 border of Armenian habitation usually was south of Lake Van, near Mush (in Armenia), and Bairt and Dersim (in Turkey). Each religion had a different status under the former Ottoman Empire—Moslems first class and conscripted into the military; all other religions, not conscripted, but taxed.

Step 2: Narrow the Categories

Categorize the religion—not only Catholic, but Melkite Catholic or Maronite Catholic. Antiochian Syrian Orthodox or Roman Catholic? Byzantine Catholic (Byzantic) or Greek Orthodox? Lebanese immigrant to Cairo, Egypt and Coptic Orthodox? Moslem? Jewish? Druze? Armenian Apostolic? Sephardim? Ashkenazim? Protestant? Greek Orthodox? Greek Catholic? Bulgarian or Romanian Orthodox? Serbian? Croatian?

Color-code cards or files noting the date, religion, ethnic group, and town. When did the immigrant arrive in the US from a Middle Eastern country? Was it before or after the end of the former Ottoman Empire? For example, Antioch, now in Turkey used to be in Syria before World War II. And before 1918, Syria and Lebanon was one province under the Ottoman Empire. So use old and new **maps** to see what country to emphasize at which dates.

Step 3: National Archives in the Country of Origin

Maps of old neighborhoods show locations of houses. Start with the national archives in the country of origin. For Syria that would be the Syrian National Archives in Damascus, Aleppo, Homs, or Hama where court records are archived for the years 1517 to 1919. If the relatives lived before the end of the Ottoman Empire or before World War I, also search the census records of the former Ottoman Empire in Turkey rather than the archives in the country of origin that may not have existed before the end of the Ottoman Empire.

Records stand alone rather than in groups of catalogs. Check separate Jewish genealogy sources and synagogue documents for the Jewish records of Mizrahi and Sephardim, such as marriage ketubim, bar mitzvah records, births, deaths, rabbinical documents such as a 'Get' for a divorce or a pedigree called a Yiccus.

If you're checking Sephardic (Jewish) records of the former Ottoman Empire, there's an excellent article on Jewish genealogy published in Los Muestros maga-zine, a publication of Sephardic and Middle Eastern Jewish genealogy titled Resources for Sephardic Genealogy at: http://www.sefarad.org/publication/lm/010/cardoza.html. Also see the magazine, Los Muestros at: http://www.sefarad.org/publication/lm/010/som10.html for archived Sephardic genealogy articles.

Another excellent publication of Jewish genealogy, Avotaynu maintains a Web site at: http://www.avotaynu.com/. If you're looking for Jewish records in the Middle East, also check the Sephardic associations, for example, Sephardim.com at http://www.sephardim.com/. Look for memorabilia, diaries, house keys, and maps of neighborhoods.

For Sephardic genealogy in the former Ottoman Empire, contact the Founda-tion for the Advancement of Sephardic Studies and Culture Web site at: http://www.sephardicstudies.org/cal2.html to learn how to interpret calendars and how to read birth certificates. You'll learn how to decipher the handwritten entries using Arabic script. Regardless of the religion of the individual, this site shows you how to read the certificates written with certain types of scripts.

The site also shows the dialects spoken in the various areas of the Ottoman Empire. Also there is information on how to read the Arabic script but Turkish language writing on gravestones, especially in Turkish cemeteries. The site shows you how to read the alphabet encountered in genealogical research in the former Ottoman Empire. Emphasis is on interpreting Sephardic birth certificates.

Step 4: How to Translate and Locate without Surnames

What's in the census? Ottoman census records for the period 1831–1872 were compilations of male names and addresses for fiscal and military purposes. Instead of population counts, the Ottoman records contain the name of the head of household, male family members, ages, occupation, and property.

You won't find surnames in old records. Most Middle Eastern countries didn't require surnames until after the fall of the Ottoman Empire. If you're searching Middle Eastern genealogy before 1924, begin by familiarizing yourself with the record keeping and social history of the Ottoman Empire.

Turkish language written in Arabic script is the key to searching genealogy records in European and Middle Eastern areas formerly ruled by the Ottomans. You'll need an Arabic-English dictionary or instruction guide that at least gives you the basic Arabic script alphabet.

You'll also need the same type of phrase book with alphabet translation for modern Turkish written using Latin letters. You can put the both together to figure out phrases.

Find in your town a graduate student or teacher from abroad who reads Arabic script and modern Turkish. Hire the student or teacher to copy the records you want when overseas. Barter services. Or contact the Middle East history and area studies, archaeology, or languages departments of numerous colleges.

Who teaches courses in both Turkish and Arabic? Contact private language schools such as Language School International, Inc. at: http://www.languageschoolsguide.com/listingsp3.cfm/listing/4092.

Step 5: What Religious Group Will You Search?

Social history is the key to genealogy. Records that existed under the Ottoman Empire listed names of the head of household and parents, residence, dates and places of birth and baptism, marriage, death and burial. Records also have entries for ages for marriage and death.

Baptisms included names of the godparents. Deaths sometimes included the cause of death. For Christians, entries sometimes identified residence for those not of the parish. Check the state archives in the country of your ancestors and also in Turkey. Then check the court, notary, and property records.

Contact the parish churches to look at parish registers and synagogues to look at the Jewish registers. If you're checking Bulgaria, Macedonia, or Greece, numerous pre-1872 registers are located in Greece. "The Bulgarian Orthodox Church was subordinate to the Patriarchate in Greece before 1872," notes researcher, Khalile Mehr. Find out whether a country had its state church subordinate to another country's church with records archived in a different language. An excellent reference book is titled,

Step 6: Check Business, School Alumni, Medical, Military, Marriage, and Property Records

Research wills and marriage records in order to track down property records. Search medical and dental records, hospitals, orphanages, prisons, asylums, midwives' records, marriage certificates, business licenses, work permits, migration papers, passports, military pensions, notaries, sales records of homes or businesses, or any other court, military, or official transaction that might have occurred.

If you're Armenian, check out the Turkish Armenian Reconciliation Commission (TARC) at: http://www.asbarez.com/TARC/Tarc.html. Or for the Balkans, look at the Center for Democracy and Reconciliation in Southeast Europe's Web site at: http://www.cdsee.org/teaching_packs_belgrade_bio.html.

Step 7: Search the 'Annual' Census and the Population Registers

Check recorded births and deaths in the first Ottoman census of 1831. Each census focused on tabulating male names to find Moslem men to conscript into the military service known as "The Army." Before 1881, the annual census registered only the male population. Search the names of committee members.

Committees were set up each year to register the males in order to keep tabs on migrations in and out of each district. When the census wasn't taken, the Population Register of Moslem males kept careful records of migrations.

Find out in which local district or 'kaza' your ancestor lived. Ottomans called their annual census the sicil-i nüfus after 1881 or the nüfus between 1831–1850. You can research the **Ottoman Census and Population Registers** named in Turkish the **Nüfus Defter**. Ottoman population demographics and statistics adjusted to satisfy tax desires, since the non-Moslem population was taxed but not conscripted into military service.

The annual census didn't cover every year. Check the Ottoman census for the years1881–1883, and 1903–1906. Family historians can search each census as well as separate registers to view supplemental registration of births, marriages, divorces, and deaths.

After 1881, the census takers counted all individuals (not only Moslem males) in the census and in the population registers. Sometimes people who thought all genealogy records were destroyed in fires in their native country are surprised to learn that census records may be archived far away in Turkey. If you need text or a Web site translated into numerous languages, check out the Systran Web site at: http://www.systranbox.com/systran/box. You can translate free an entire Web site or 150 words of text.

◆   ◆   ◆

Armenian Genealogy

Check out these resources on the Web: The Armenian Research List is an on-line posting of Armenian genealogy and family history questions and answers at: http://feefhs.org/am/frg-amgs.html. Go to the Armenia Genealogy Forum. Check out this small group of dedicated Armenian-Americans that are actively engaged in seeking out Armenian records for preservation through microfilming and in assisting the formation of the first Armenian Family History Center (in-country) at Yeravan. If you want to research resources about Jews in medieval Armenia, check out the Web site at: http://www.khazaria.com/armenia/armenian-jews.html.

Then go to the **Armenian Research List** at: http://feefhs.org/am/amrl.html. The Armenian Research List is an on-line posting of Armenian genealogy and family history questions and answers. If you have Armenian ancestry, you are encouraged to submit your own summary genealogy and your questions. Go to the Armenian surnames as well as given male and female names at: http://feefhs.org/am/frg-amgs.html.

Search the **Armenian Apostolic Church Parish Records. Then click on the online Armenia Genealogy** Forum at: http://genforum.genealogy.com/armenia/ . You can also search Armenian genealogy resources at http://www.DistantCousin.com. Check out genforum.genealogy.com/Armenia/ and also http://www.distantcousin.com/Links/Ethnic/Armenia/.

An Armenian genealogy Web site also is at: http:// www.geocities.com/Paris/Palais/2230/index2.html. Search Armenian genealogy at: **genealogy**.freewebsitehosting.com/ links/**armeniangenealogy**. And links to Armenian genealogy resources Web sites are at: www.rootsweb.com/~armwgw/links.html. Then go to the Genealogy Register: Armenia at: http://genealogyregister.com/Asia/Armenia/. You'll find there these wonderful links to resources for searching Armenian genealogy such as the following: Family trees, the Armenia Genealogy Forum. It's a list of postings where Armenians having lost their relatives during the deportations and the genocide search members of their families and their descendants. The site features also a chat room.

The Armenia Research List contains postings by individuals who search information about lost family members during the genocide. There is also an archive. Click on Armeniagenweb at: http://www.rootsweb.com/~armwgw/. It has links to Armenian mailing lists and surname pages. You'll also find at the Armenian Genealogical Society. an Armenian research list and lists of Armenian names and surnames.

For passenger lists of ships transporting immigrations, check out the Armenian Genealogical Web Page. It also has a bibliography, and presents the book of a genealogist, cemetery data, maps, genocide survivor stories, information about Armenian legionnaires during World War I.

The Distant Cousins: Armenian Genealogy Resources Features an Armenian surname search engine, a list of web resources and mailing lists, links for Armenian family historians including books and personal homepages. You can also read the Family Questionnaire. It's provided by the Armenian Historical Association of Rhode Island. The questionnaire is intended for determining the contribution of Armenians to the history of Rhode Island.

You need various personal and family data to answer the questionnaire. There's also a link to a genealogist specializing in Armenian research. All these informational links are at the Genealogy Register at: http://genealogyregister.com/Asia/Armenia/. There are surname lists and a home page.

Check it out. I highly rate and recommend this Web site for Armenian genealogy resources research. Click on the link to the Armenia Genealogy Forum at: http://genealogyregister.com/Asia/Armenia/. It has a list of postings where relatives may search for the descendants of lost and deported family members' names.

◆　　◆　　◆

Web Resources and Books on Former Ottoman Empire Genealogy Web Sites

Albanian Research List: http://feefhs.org/al/alrl.html

Armenian Genealogical Society: http://feefhs.org/am/frg-amgs.html

Egyptian Genealogy: http://www.daddezio.com/egypgen.html
Egyptian Genealogy—Kindred Trails (tm): http://www.kindredtrails.com/egypt.html

Egyptian Royal Genealogy: http://www.geocities.com/christopherjbennett/

Historical Society of Jews from Egypt: http://www.hsje.org/homepage.htm

Iranian: Persian Watch Center: Iranian-American AntiDiscrimination Council http://www.antidiscrimination.org/

The Iranian:
http://www.iranian.com/Features/2002/December/LA2/index.html

Iran: Payvand's Iran News: http://www.payvand.com/news/00/aug/1054.html

Also see: Iranian American Jewish Federation and also the Council of Iranian American Jewish Organizations: P.O.BOX 3074, Beverly Hills, CA. 90212. See news article at Payvand's Iran News at: http://www.payvand.com/news/00/feb/1014.html

Excellent Genealogy and Related Books on Iran: Also see: http://payvand.com/books/

Another Sea, Another Shore: Stories of Iranian Migration
by Shouleh Vatanabadi, et all (2003)

Funny in Farsi: A Memoir of Growing Up Iranian in America
by Firoozeh Dumas (2003)

Wedding Song: Memoirs of an Iranian Jewish Woman
by Farideh Goldin (2003)

Exiled Memories: Stories of the Iranian Diaspora
by Zohreh Sullivan (2001)

Journey from the Land of No : A Girlhood Caught in Revolutionary Iran
by Roya Hakakian (2004)

Inside Iran: Women's Lives
by Jane Mary Howard (2002)

The National Iranian American Council: www.niacouncil.org

Jewish Genealogy: http://www.jewishgen.org/infofiles/

Lebanon Genealogy: http://genforum.genealogy.com/lebanon

http://www.mit.edu:8001/activities/lebanon/map.html

Lebanese Descendants of the Bourjaily Family (Abou R'Jaily): http://www.abourjeily.com/Family/index.htm
Descendants of Atallah Abou Rjeily, born about 1712

Lebanese Club of New York City:
http://nyc.lebaneseclub.org/
http://www.rootsweb.com/~lbnwgw/lebclubnyc/index.htm

Lebanese Genealogy: http://www.rootsweb.com/~lbnwgw/

Middle East Genealogy: http://www.rootsweb.com/~mdeastgw/index.html

Middle East Genealogy by country: http://www.rootsweb.com/~mdeastgw/index.html#country

Polish Genealogical Society of America: http://feefhs.org/pol/frg-pgsa.html

Sephardim.com: http://www.sephardim.com/

Syrian and Lebanese Genealogy: http://www.genealogytoday.com/family/syrian/

Syria Genealogy: http://www.rootsweb.com/~syrwgw/

Syrian/Lebanese/Jewish/Farhi Genealogy Site (Flowers of the Orient): http://www.farhi.org

Turkish Genealogy Discussion Group: http://www.turkey. com/forums/forumdisplay.php3?forumid=18

Turkish Telephone Directories Information: Türk Telekomünikasyon (Telecommunication) http://ttrehber.gov.tr/rehber_webtech/index.asp

Croatia Genealogy Cross Index: http://feefhs.org/cro/indexcro.html

Eastern Europe: http://www.cyndislist.com/easteuro.htm

Eastern European Genealogical Society, Inc.: http://feefhs.org/ca/frg-eegs.html

Eastern Europe Index: http://feefhs.org/ethnic.html

India Royalty: http://freepages.genealogy.rootsweb.com/~royalty/india/persons.html

Romanian American Heritage Center: http://feefhs.org/ro/frg-rahc.html

Slavs, South: Cultural Society: http://feefhs.org/frg-csss.html

Ukrainian Genealogical and Historical Society of Canada: http://feefhs.org/ca/frgughsc.html

Rom (Gypsies): http://www.cyndislist.com/peoples.htm#Gypsies

See: McGowan, Bruce William, 1933- **Defter-i mufassal-i liva-i Sirem : an Ottoman revenue survey dating from the reign of Selim II./ Bruce William McGowan.**
Ann Arbor, Mich.: University Microfilms, 1967.

See: **Bogaziçi University** Library Web sites:
http://seyhan.library.boun.edu.tr/search/wN{232}ufus+Defter/
wN{232}ufus+Defter/1,29,29,B/frameset&FF=wN{232}ufus+Defter&9,9,

or http://seyhan.library.boun.edu.tr/search/dTaxation+—+Turkey.
/dtaxation+turkey/-5,-1,0,B/exact&FF=dtaxation+turkey&1,57,

Jurisdictions and localities in Bulgaria:
Michev N. and P. Koledarov. *Rechnik na selishchata i selishchnite imena v Bulgariia, 1878–1987* (Dictionary of villages and village names in Bulgaria, 1878–1987), Sofia: Nauka i izkustvo, 1989 (FHL book 949.77 E5m).

2

Searching Genealogy Records in Macedonia of the Former Ottoman Empire

The material on Macedonia Bulgaria, and Croatia is copyrighted by the Family History Library, and the information was sent to me by its author, former staff writer for the Family History Library, Mr. Khalile Mehr. From this material, the information on Bulgaria, Macedonia, and Croatia has been summarized. For further information, consult the Family History Library as they have excellent sources of information on genealogy in these Balkan countries.

Acknowledgement and thanks is to Mr. Mehr and the Family History Library. Hungarian material was sent to me by its author, Anthony Trendl, Community Editor, the Hungarian Bookstore.

Start with parish registers. Then proceed to civil registration and the censuses. Since most of the Christian population of Macedonia is Macedonian Orthodox, which is similar to Serbian Orthodox, if you're searching parish registers from 1800 to the present, you can probably find records from 1800 forwards in time in the parish registers. You'll find the parish registers in the national, historical, and community archives as well as in various churches.

If you're looking for civil registration, there wasn't any until 1946. For dates before 1913, look to the Ottoman population registers, because after 1913 Macedonia was then part of Serbia. Write to the Ministry of Internal Affairs to look through civil registration materials. The Ministry of Internal Affairs is not the state archives.

Your next step would be to turn to the censuses. They were under the Ottoman population registers before 1913. When the Ottoman Empire fell, Macedonia became part of Serbia. Therefore, 1921 became the year of the first national census at the time that Macedonia then became an area within Yugoslavia.

Next you'll want to turn to the Ottoman population registers. You can find the census returns/population registers from 1829 or 1831. When you skip to 1881–1889, you'll find that by that time the records have been meticulously swept within a single system. You'll view the census returns at the district level (kaza).

At first only Moslem males were registered, but the information portrays a vivid picture as described because not only are the birth dates recorded or the migrations in and out, but also eye color and complexion down to the freckles. You'll note that what was recorded included whether they moved, date of death, and military service dates.

When you get to the 1881 census and later tabulations of population, you'll see that the goal was to establish a demography or population figures for political and social history. Not only Moslem males, but all people were then counted in both the census and the population registers after that date.

The registers listed all family members; sex; birth date; residence; age; religion; craft or occupation; marital status, marriage date; health; military status. It's a good way to find out the religion or occupation of family members.

Your third step would be to turn to records in the Family History Library collection. According to the Library, "Virtually no manuscript materials have been filmed by the Family History Library." If your family comes from one of the countries under the former Ottoman Empire, it would be great if you can donate manuscript materials to be filmed. Ask them first if they are accepting materials and in what form.

Research Procedures

The catalog of the Family History Library may have records listed by the name of the district or the town. According to the Family History Library, look for jurisdictions and localities in Slovenia by consulting a book of place names in the former Yugoslavia. The Family History Library in Salt Lake City refers researchers to the book titled: *Imenik mesta u Jugoslaviji* (Places names in Yugoslavia). Beograd: Novinska Ustanova Sluñbeni List SFRJ, 1973. (949.7 E5u; film 874,462 item 2)

Have you researched records at the national level? If so, look for records from a specific town or area. The films are not housed in the Family History Library.

Order films prior to arriving in Salt Lake City by calling or writing: Family History Library, Attn: Library Attendants, 35 N. West Temple Street, Salt Lake City, UT 84150-3400, telephone: 801-240-2331.

War, earthquakes, and fire have destroyed lots of Macedonian archives and records. You have to tend with the destruction of documents from the Balkan wars as well as World War I and II. What if you had to search the ancient library at Alexandria? Yet all is not lost.

Between 1918 and 1941, you can search the state archive in Beograd for genealogy records in what was called Macedonia when your relatives lived there.

World War II devastated the archives of Skopje. The Archive of Macedonia was established in 1951. It has a website at http://www.arhiv.gov.mk/Ang1.htm. You'll have to allow for the 1963 earthquake that demolished the facility, but a new building rose in 1969. What you can search there are nine regional archives located in Bitola, Kumanovo, Ohrid, Prilep, Skopje, Strumica, Tetovo, Titov Veles, and Stip. What genealogy records that remain at the Archive of Macedonia includes mostly material from after 1969. Therefore, it's wise to check with them to see whether anything exists from a former period.

If you're researching religion, in 1870 the newly established Bulgarian exarchate received the support of Macedonians, mainly because of its Slavic character. In 1958, the Macedonian Orthodox Church was reestablished in Ohrid. So Macedonia broke free of the Ottoman Empire during the Balkan wars of 1912–1913. Searching records could include tracking relatives to Greece, Bulgaria, or Serbia as Macedonia was divided between Serbia and Greece with a tiny part going to Bulgaria.

Find out whether your relatives lived in Aegean Macedonia (Greece), Vardar Macedonia (Serbia), or Pirin Macedonia (Bulgaria). After 1991, land-locked Macedonia became a small, independent nation. Records could be difficult to find, but also may be hidden in church parishes and family keepsakes. Some records along with religious items were sewn inside of clothing, quilt, and drapery hems. So check out your relatives' oral histories and traditions.

3

Croatia Genealogy Research

First look at the Family History Library's microfilm collection on Croatia. They have about 2,600 rolls of microfilm that were sent in from Croatia since filming began there in 1985. Filming has occurred at the central state archive and regional archives of Osijek, Varañdin, Zadar, Split, Dubrovnik, Rijeka, and Pazin. **The material on Macedonia Bulgaria, and Croatia is copyrighted by the Family History Library, and the information was sent to me by its author, former staff writer for the Family History Library, Mr. Khalile Mehr. From this material, the information on Bulgaria, Macedonia, and Croatia has been summarized. For further information, consult the Family History Library as they have excellent sources of information on genealogy in these Balkan countries.**

Acknowledgement and thanks is to Mr. Mehr and the Family History Library. Hungarian material was sent to me by its author, Anthony Trendl, Community Editor, the Hungarian Bookstore.

If you're looking at parish registers, they start in the 1700s and are archived until the present. Roman Catholic parishes kept registers earlier than Orthodox parishes which were required to keep them only after 1777.

According to the Family History Library, "Civil transcripts of registers were mandated during the 19th century. A tabular format was adopted after 1848. In 1946, civil registration replaced parish registration of vital events.

As of 1945 most registers were turned over to civil authorities and deposited in the local city hall. Older registers have been and continue to be transferred to the district historical archives or the Croatia State Archive."

To find the registers, contact the Civil Registry offices. If you need post World War Two material from the Civil Registers—after 1946, they are there. However, civil registration before May 1946 contains the names and data on Moslems only. After 1946, civil authorities in Croatia and the rest of Yugoslavia began universal registration.

Next, look at the censuses that start in the year 1785 and continue until the present.

During the Ottoman Empire, the census followed the usual name-taking for taxation or conscription and to provide a demography of the people in Croatia.

If you want military records of ancestors, the first military census began in 1785. By 1804-5, you have the civil census. Regular censuses were conducted in 1857, 1869, and every ten years, 1880–1910. Go to the archives of each district or city to find a name lists if it is available.

The Family History Library in Salt Lake City recommends for searching genealogy records of Croatia the book titled ***Imenik mesta u Jugoslaviji*** (Places names in Yugoslavia). Beograd: Novinska Ustanova Sluñibeni List SFRJ, 1973. (949.7 E5u; film 874,462 item 2)

This book will help you to identify the jurisdictions and localities. If you can't read the place names in Yugoslavia, then check out the Family History Library Catalog to see if any records are listed under the name of the town or the district.

Your next step would be to search records on a national level. Look for specific towns or villages and cities. The films are not housed in the Family History Library. Order films prior to arriving in Salt Lake City by calling or writing: Family History Library, Attn: Library Attendants, 35 N. West Temple Street, Salt Lake City, UT 84150-3400, telephone: 801-240-2331.

If you've exhausted the Croatian social associations in the US, then turn to the Croatia State Archive, Hrvatski Dravni Arhiv, Maruliev Trg. 21, 10000 Zagreb, telephone: 385-01-4801-930, fax 385-01-4829-000, email hda@arhiv.hr, web http://zagreb.arhiv.hr/.

Instead of actually going to the country in person, email first to set up appointments where you'll go if you actually make a trip over there.

Old books were transferred to the archives in 1957—that means books more than 1000 years old. Check out the town halls because they have registers dating before World War II.

After the war, the churches kept registers. There was a census in 1957. If you're looking for old records before 1857, then go to archives at the church registers as well as the state archives. A lot of registers remain in parishes.

Look for transcripts in the Archbishopric Archive. According to the Family History Library, "Pedigrees are scattered in the collection. Though censuses were conducted in 1857, 1869, 1880, 1890, and 1900, there are no census records in the archive."

The charge 88 kuna/hour for research. There are twelve district historical archives and contact information is available on the web site. Check out the Zagreb Historical Archive. Historijski arhiv Zagreb, Opati...ka 29, 10000 Zagreb, telephone: 385-01-4551-375, fax 385-01-4851-374, <u>povijesni-arhiv-zg@zg.tel.hr</u>, open 9:00-14:00 daily. The Family History Library notes that "A good genealogy website is found at: <u>http://www.croatia-in-english.com/gen/index.html</u>."

There are numerous Croatian social halls and associations in the USA and other countries because more than a quarter of all Croatians lived outside of Croatia by 1970. Check these social and fraternal or family associations for genealogy connections and books, published or unpublished, written by individuals for their own families.

Croats are mainly Roman Catholic, and speak Croatian, and Serbs are mostly Orthodox and speak Serbian. The language of the records are either Latin, Croatian, Hungarian, or Italian. Besides Roman script, there is also Glagolitic script.

4

Genealogy Records in Bulgaria, Hungary, and Eastern Europe Under the Former Ottoman Empire

The material on Macedonia Bulgaria, and Croatia is copyrighted by the Family History Library, and the information was sent to me by its author, former staff writer for the Family History Library, Mr. Khalile Mehr. From this material, the information on Bulgaria, Macedonia, and Croatia has been summarized. For further information, consult the Family History Library as they have excellent sources of information on genealogy in these Balkan countries.

Acknowledgement and thanks is to Mr. Mehr and the Family History Library. Hungarian material was sent to me by its author, Anthony Trendl, Community Editor, the Hungarian Bookstore.

Check out the Bulgaria Genealogy forum at: http://genforum.genealogy.com/bulgaria/. If you're Jewish, also check out the Sephardi Connection Discussion Forums People Finder at the Sephardi Connection. Their Web site is at: http://sephardiconnect.com/webx/webx.cgi?sephard-13@%5E185@.ee6c850.

If you're Christian, look at the Orthodox and Catholic records which date back to around 1850. A few Catholic books go back to slightly before 1797. These genealogy records have the names of the head of household and parents, residence, dates and places of birth and baptism, marriage, death and burial; as well as ages in entries for marriage and death.

According to the Family History Library in Salt Lake City, baptisms include names of the godparents. Deaths sometimes include the cause of death.

Entries sometimes identify residence for those not of the parish. Some parish registers have been sent to the state archives or the national museum. Visit the parish churches to look at parish registers.

Some pre-1872 registers are in Greece. Before 1872 the Bulgarian Orthodox Church was subordinate to the Patriarchate in Greece. If you're looking for civil registration, the records begin around 1893 when the process of civil registration began.

According to the Family History Library, "Birth, marriage, and death records have the exact date of the event, including time of day for births; name of the principal and parents' names; occupation and religious preference of parents; name of informant for births and witnesses for marriages; residence for parents of new born, of the groom and bride for marriages, and of the deceased for deaths; age at death, cause of death, and burial place in death records."

Go to the district archives in each of the 26 districts of Bulgaria to find specific records for particular areas. To record all the vital information in the same building, in 1920 family registers came into practice.

To find these family registers before 1920, look to the national census. It began in 1880. The first national census took place right after Bulgaria's liberation from Ottoman rule.

Because 19th century name lists are not available, you'd have to turn to the Ottoman census records for the period 1831–1872. Only these records were enumerations of males for tax, fiscal, and military purposes. They contain the name of the head of household, male family members, ages, occupation, and property.

To start with the Family History Library, go to their small book collection and microfilms of civil registration, 1893–1906, for the Bulgarian districts of Sofia and Pazardzhik. You're going to have to list the local areas or jurisdictions to narrow down your search. To find these jurisdictions, you need the book by Michev N. and P. Koledarov. *Rechnik na selishchata i selishchnite imena v Bulgariia, 1878–1987* (Dictionary of villages and village names in Bulgaria, 1878–1987), Sofia: Nauka i izkustvo, 1989 (FHL book 949.77 E5m).

Once you have the name of the district and town, go to the Family History Library Catalog (Salt Lake City). There may be records listing under the name of the district in Bulgaria. If you can't find anything, then check national level records of a specific town rather than the district.

You can see some of these towns on films. The films are not housed in the Family History Library. Order films prior to arriving in Salt Lake City by calling or writing: Family History Library, Attn: Library Attendants, 35 N. West Temple Street, Salt Lake City, UT 84150-3400, telephone: 801-240-2331.

To narrow down the districts, there are only twenty six. In each of the districts, there is an archive. In that archive you have church records and civil registration records. Then narrow down still more as you go to the churches and monasteries.

You won't find vital records in the National Historical Archive in Sofia, according to the Family History Library research. A guide exists to the holdings of this archive: ***Putevoditel na Tsentralniia Durzhaven Istoricheski Arkhiv,*** Sofia: Nauka i izkustvo, 1970 (FHL book 949.77 A5p).

To research deeper, turn to the Ottoman census records at the Oriental Department of the Cyril and Methodius National Library, Sofia. What if you don't read Bulgarian? If you get to the records at the Cyril and Methodius National Library, find a translator or translation manual and then go onto the next nation in nearby Istanbul.

Once in Istanbul, look at the archives of the Ottoman Empire. You've now reached the core of the former Ottoman Empire. It seems everything lands up in Istanbul, or does it? That depends on what else is in the various churches or synagogues depending upon your ethnic identity or religion. Check out the genealogy site on the Web at: www.rootsweb.com/~bgrwgw/index.html#NEW.

When searching Bulgaria, understand it was the first state to join the Ottoman Empire and the last to be liberated. Bulgaria was under the former Ottoman Empire from 1396–1878, only to be liberated by the Russian army. Another country was added to Bulgaria called Eastern Rumelia, in the southeast.

More territory was added by 1913 during the Balkan wars. A lot of records were hidden because Bulgaria allied with Germany in both World Wars. So if you're of ethnic groups whose records were hidden, such as Sephardic Jews, you need to go to synagogues and Sephardic organizations to find links and leads to where the records can be found. In 1990 Bulgaria became an independent country.

Records are kept in different places for different ethnic groups. You have besides Bulgaries, the Rom people (Gypsies), Turks, Macedonians, Armenians, Russians and Sephardic Jews. If you need to learn Bulgarian before searching records, the Slavic language is written in Cyrillic script.

When you search records, the languages will change with the ethnicity of the people being recorded. Records are found not only in Bulgarian, the main language, but also in Turkish, Greek, and Old Church Slavonic as well as the Sephardic records of synagogues and Jewish schools in Hebrew and Judezmo/ Ladino. Acknowledgement and credit for this information on Bulgaria, Croatia, and Macedonia is given to the Family History Library, Salt Lake City, UT.

Hungary

Start your search of genealogy records for Hungry when it was under the former Ottoman Empire by going to the Hungarian Bookstore site on the Web at: http://www.hungarianbookstore.com/. They have links to many Hungarian sites and publications. Join various Hungarian associations.

These include the American Hungarian Foundation, the American Hungarian Library and Historical Society, and the various Hungarian Genealogy Societies in your locality. Contact the Carpatho-Rusyn Society. Gather your maps.

You can also contact the Hungarian Genealogy of Greater Cleveland and the Cleveland Hungarian Heritage Museum, if you're visiting Ohio. Then look at the Hungarian Phone Book if you can read Hungarian. Search for familiar surnames. Look in the Budapest City Archives, the National Archives of Hungary, the HungaryGenWeb, and the Map pages of Eötvös University, Department of Cartography. If you go to the Hungarian Bookstore Web site at: http://www.hungarianbookstore.com/, you'll find links to various genealogy Web sites and even a Hungarian language radio station.

It's a good start to join a Hungarian or Hungarian-American group and also to subscribe to a magazine from your ancestor's town. Check out the Web site on East European genealogy at: http://www.feefhs.org/. Or if you can write in Hungarian, consider joining soc.culture.magyar, a Google newsgroup online. It's at: http://groups.google.com/groups?hl=en&lr=&ie=UTF-8&oe=UTF-8&group=soc.culture.magyar.

According to email from Anthony Trendl, community editor, **The Hungarian Bookstore**, I asked the following question: Where would be the best place to start to search Hungarian genealogy if one only speaks English? Mr. Trendl's answer by email is the following:

Anne,

That's a big question. :)

My caveat is I'm not a professional genealogist. We're still getting into this ourselves. My dad's side is Hungarian (I'm American), and my fiancée is from Hungary. I only speak English, and have the same handicap as those in your book.

The wars and such have chopped up the country, and in some cases, destroyed records. Don't be discouraged. There is still hope.

Some of what it takes to research Hungarian genealogy is logical, and useful in any genealogical project. Here's what's off the top of my head.

- The most obvious start is to talk to everyone in your family. This isn't always easy, since most have never been interviewed and aren't used to thinking what you, the reporter might want to know. Bring a tape recorder. Follow-up with new questions.

- Watch History Detectives on PBS. These sharp sleuths have little to do with genealogy, but they do research in the same kind of creative manner that you will find helpful.

- Be organized in your research. Label things, scan things, and start connecting the dots. As your work grows, so will your files. Good organization can keep a researcher from going batty later on.

- Make copies of everyone in your family's baptismal, wedding, and death records.

- Do some reading on the communities from where you think you came from. There are plenty of good resources for history out there.

- Remember communism revised some of the history books to suit their views. Look at the book's copyright date. Suspect anything before 1989.

- Remember religion in Hungary is largely cultural. Don't presume that just because someone claims to be Catholic, for example, that they've ever been actually involved in the parish serving that area. Also, some Jews converted rather than be killed.

- As country lines have change, recognize sometimes city names have changed as well. In doing some reading…even starting with the local library's travel guides, you'll start to get a feel for an area. Some are more English-speaking than others.

- Remember the Holocaust hit Hungarians hard. It wasn't just Jews, but those suspected of being Jewish, and those who simply were Hungarian.

- Go to Hungary. Research your tail off, save all of it on a CD, and come on over to Hungary to do more. Plan ahead, and have an itinerary and meetings planned. If it is a social trip, just be sure to be disciplined. Hungary is beautiful, and it is easy to get sidetracked.

- When you go to Hungary, bring your camera and have unlimited film. Ask permission when inside places.

- Take pictures of your relatives.

- Churches can be a great asset. Baptisms, weddings, all that sort of thing often are recorded. Even though you may not read Hungarian, learning a few key words to understand headings can help.

- Buy a dictionary that covers both languages. Get a real one, not one of those travel ones. You want to learn the word for "baptism' not 'bathroom' :)

- Find a Hungarian friend willing to help.

- Consider hiring a translation service. We used one here in Chicago to translate medical records while we prepared papers for INS.

- When surfing the web, you can still use Hungarian sites. Many have English versions. Look for the little Britiish flag.

- Google has a Hungarian version. That's no small thing, since it can help you isolate your research.

- Surnames change. Not only do people drop accents from their name, but occasionally, the spelling changes. In America, you might find Kovach, but in Hungary, it is likely spelled Kovacs. Same pronunciation, different spelling.

- Join a genealogy club. Eastern Europe is more than just Hungary, but there are lots from Eastern and Central Europe roots who have already tread the path you are starting on. Don't be shy. Ask questions.

My site has a genealogy section that includes lots of links to official city sites in Hungary, like for Pecs and Szeged. You'll also see a number of useful books, software applications and magazines, all available for purchase.

http://www.hungarianbookstore.com/**genealogy**.htm   (Genealogy links—including online discussion boards, plus a short essay)

http://www.hungarianbookstore.com/**language**.htm (Dictionaries, tips, and some online dictionary links readers can use for free)

http://www.hungarianbookstore.com/**news**.htm   (Magazines, newspapers…very useful for the researcher looking to know the culture. Many are in English).

http://www.hungarianbookstore.com/**groups**.htm (Listing of Hungarian social clubs in the USA, including online discussion boards. Very useful for researchers trying to learn about the ins and outs of the country. They can also be a great resource to find professional assistance.)

I'm interested in reading your book when is ready. I also review on Amazon, and am ranked among their top reviewers. The link below will take you to my area on Amazon. Contact me again to get a current address if you'd like to send a review copy. I review nonHungarian-related books as well, so don't be surprised to see my thoughts on the latest bestseller next to a book on Hungarian poetry. :)

About HungarianBooks editor@hungarianbookstore.com

I hope this helps you Anne. Feel free to quote me as you like, and reference our site when you do.

Anthony Trendl
community editor
editor@hungarianbookstore.com
The Hungarian Bookstore
http://www.hungarianbookstore.com

The Hungarian Bookstore connects Hungarians with their culture by providing a directory of churches, restaurants and grocery stores. We sell books, DVDs, CDs, music, videos, magazines, newspapers and more.

◆   ◆   ◆

Searching Several Areas Formerly Under the Ottoman Empire

If your relatives lived under the former Ottoman Empire in Hungary, Yugoslavia, Croatia, Bosnia, Albania, Macedonia, Greece, Romania, Moldova, Bulgaria, southern Ukraine, Turkey, Georgia, Armenia, Iraq, Kuwait, Cyprus, Syria, Lebanon, Israel/Palestine, Jordan, Eastern and Western Saudi Arabia, Oman, Bahrain, eastern Yemen, Egypt, northern Libya, Tunisia, and northern Algeria, the first step to take after gathering your own family or client's materials such as birth, marriage, and death certificates, military service, or maps of old addresses and towns is to join associations and subscribe to magazines about that area of the world.

Whether your relatives or clients had ancestors who came from Albania, Romania, Moldova, Cyprus, Syria, Egypt, Yemen, Libya, Tunisia, Northern Algeria or any of the European countries under the Ottoman Empire before 1914, you gather your materials and start your search in pretty much the same way.

You look at church parishes, synagogues, mosques, religious schools, public schools, marriage licenses, death certificates, birth certificates, passports, ship passenger registries, dates entered the US or Canada or any other country, and you contact people in ethnic associations.Online you search for magazines published in the town or near the city of your ancestor's or client's birth.

You look at material in the Family History Library if it's there, or you go to the various genealogy groups for Eastern European or Middle Eastern genealogy and ancestry research. If you belong to a particular ethnic or religious group you go to records kept by your ethnic or religious group.

Jewish genealogy records would be kept in different places than Christian records in most of the countries under the Ottoman Empire, but not always and not in every country. So check out individual town registers as they may not have classified always by religion. Some countries had population registers for all males or heads of households and for all family members.

Other countries recorded the migrations in and out of the country, and still other countries kept a record of what the person looked like, military service, and property ownership for tax collection purposes or notary recordings. So check notaries and court records as well as wills and recorded marriages.

Some people migrated from one country that was under the Ottoman Empire to a country that wasn't. For example, back-migration from Romania to Poland or Ukraine. If you're Sephardic, a good source is Sephardim.com at: http://www.sephardim.com/. Search their engine for surnames.

The Sephardic names search engine lists names going back to the 14th century and beyond by alphabet letter. For example, the name Leven, a Sephardic name in the 14th century, shows up later as an Ashkenazi name (Levin/Levine/Lewin) in Poland in the 18th century and also showing a migration to Bessarabia, Romania, in the late 18th century coming from Poland.

Another excellent site is Sephardic Genealogy Forum at: http://www.orthohelp.com/geneal/sources2.HTM. At that Web site you might want to check out the passenger lists of Spaniards and/or Sephardim sailing to the Americas between 1500 and 1800. The archive of passengers is still in Seville. You'll find the records in the Archivo General de Indias.

The list of passengers from each ship sailing to America up to1800, the records state each passenger name and place of birth, name of parents and their brithplaces, the job and destination of the passenger after arrival in the Americas. If you write to the archives in Seville, include the following: passenger name and the approximate date of the trip to America. Address your inquiry addressed to: **Archivo General de Indias, Avda. Constitucion s/n, SEVILLA—SPAIN.** Phone: +34-95-4500530. Fax: +34-95-4219485. Consult also the Sephardic Forum: http://www.jewishgen.org/sefardsig/SefardForum.htm

For information on other Jewish migrations to Palestine/Israel, write to: Batya Unterschatz, Director, Jewish Agency Bureau of Missing Relatives, P.O.Box 92, Jerusalem 91000.

Also see: Avotaynu, Publishers of Works on Jewish Genealogy (Journal and Books) at: http://www.avotaynu.com/

◆   ◆   ◆

Books to Research recommended by the Web site at Sephardim.com:

Assis: Jews in the Crown of Aragon (Part II 1328–1493); Regesta of the Cartas Reales in Archivo de la Corona de Aragon. Ginzei am olam:Central Arch Hist of Jewish People, Jerusalem

Beinart: Conversos on Trial. The Inquisition in Ciudad Real. Magnes Press, Hebrew University,Jerus. 1981

Raphael: Expulsion 1492 Chronicles. Carmi House Press

Tello: Judios de Toledo—2 Vols. Instituto B Arias Montano. Consejo Sup de inverstigacions Cientificas.

5

How to Interpret Family History & Ancestry DNA Test Results for Beginners

How many DNA testing companies will show you how to interpret DNA test results for family history or direct you to instructional materials after you have had your DNA tested? Choose a company based on previous customer satisfaction, number of markers tested, and whether the company gives you choices of how many markers you want tested. Choose a DNA-driven genealogy testing company also based on the size of its various ethnic and geographic databases, and surname projects based on DNA-driven genealogy.

Before you select a company to test your DNA, find out how many genetic markers will be tested. For the maternal line, 400 base pairs of sequences are the minimum. For the paternal line (men only) 37 markers are great, but 25 markers also should be useful.

Some companies offer a 12-marker test for surname genealogy groups at a special price. When you order a home testing kit, you'll get mouthwash or a felt-tip to rub inside your cheek and mail back. Find out how long the turnaround time is for waiting to receive your results. What is the reputation of the company.

Do they have a contract with a university lab or a private lab? Who does the testing and who is the chief geneticist at their laboratory? What research articles, if any, has that scientist written or what research studies on DNA have been performed by the person in charge of the DNA testing at the laboratory? Who owns the DNA business that contracts with the lab, and how involved in genealogy-related DNA projects and databases or services is the owner? Will the company keep in touch with you and let you know by email each time you have a DNA match?

What happens to your DNA after you test it? Is it destroyed? What projects are available for you to participate in using your DNA donation or that of relatives related to ancestry, genealogy, or family history? How much will testing cost? What other projects can you donate your DNA to offering free testing for what uses?

After your DNA sample is sent to the return address, the DNA will be sent to a university or private laboratory to be tested. A report showing your sequences of the portion of DNA tested for ancestry only will come back in about six to eight weeks. The DNA-testing company will send you the report with your sequences. Now, it's up to you to find out what the sequences mean in terms of ancestry.

When you order a DNA test, you get a code number or kit number so your name remains private. Some companies let you sign a release form to allow others to contact you or you contact them by email each time you find a match with someone who shares your exact mtDNA (maternal) or Y-chromosome (paternal) genetic markers for ancestry. The DNA tested for ancestry shows only ancestry, not any risk or disease. Women have their mtDNA tested as they don't carry a Y-chromosome. Men may have their mtDNA (maternal line) or their Y-chromosome (paternal line) tested.

According to AncestryByDNA, "We've all originated from a common ancestor that lived some 200,000 years ago. The only way to know where you came from is by reading your genetic code." What might intrigue some is taking a racial percentages test to see what percentages of which 'races' live in your very ancient or recent past.

What Will Be On The DNA Report?

You'll find your sequences on the printout that you get back from your DNA testing company, but how do you interpret your sequences for ancestry? If you want more information on interpreting sequences than you find in this article, you can start with the free online message boards on DNA genealogy such as Genealogy-DNA   Rootsweb.com   at: GENEALOGY-DNA-D-request@rootsweb.com. Or you can read a book or two for beginners on how to interpret DNA test results for family history such as my book titled, *The Beginner's Guide to Interpreting Ethnic DNA Origins for Family History*. Or for more beginning information on ancestry and DNA for genealogy buffs and, and tailoring your food and medicines to your genes, try my book titled, *Find Your Personal Adam & Eve: Make DNA-Driven Genealogy Time Capsules*, paperback. Call toll free, 1-877-823-9235 or click on http://www.iuniverse.com. You can watch my instructional (free) videos on interpreting your DNA test results for family history and ancestry or on how to write salable life stories on my Web site at http://www.newswriting.net. Before you take a DNA test, enjoy these videos and look at my book or browse excerpts on *Creative Genealogy Projects.*

Your biggest question could be, "What do you do with your DNA sequences in the field of genealogy?" You look at the ethnic databases online or find long lost relatives and email them. Then you put the DNA-for-ancestry report with the interpretations along with any genealogy information and keepsakes in your time capsule as part of social history.

You can send your DNA to a world wide database collecting the world's DNA. One such database is the Molecular Genealogy Project at the Sorenson Molecular Genealogy Foundation: The Web site is at: http://www.smgf.org/. It's a "nonprofit organization founded to build a publicly accessible genealogical database." You can contribute your DNA to their database free, but you need to have a known genealogy going back at least four generations.

Your Maternal Lineage—Mitochondrial DNA (mtDNA) and Ancestry

Since women only can be tested for mitochondrial DNA which shows only the female lineages that originated thousands of years, ago, find out how many base pairs of mtDNA will be tested. Usually the minimum is 400 base pairs of mtDNA.

If your mtDNA covers a wide area, it usually signifies that the DNA sequences are very ancient and had thousands of years to spread wide distances geographically. If your mtDNA sequences are found in a very narrow area, your mtDNA may have arisen relatively more recently.

It's the mitochondrial DNA (mtDNA) that is tested to find out your maternal line. The mtDNA is passed from mother to daughter starting with one female ancestor. That ancestor started your line of mtDNA sequences thousands of years ago. Since mtDNA mutates slowly over thousands of years, you are usually told in a report that your mtDNA sequences arose anywhere depending on the sequences from 10,000 years ago to 20,000 years ago.

How to Interpret DNA Test Results—Female

Your DNA test result will give you a letter of the alphabet called your 'haplogroup' or 'clan' as Oxford Ancestors calls it. If you're of European, Middle Eastern, (or from some parts of India) your deep maternal ancestry letters will be H,

I, J, K, N, R, T, U, V, W, or X. Most European lineages of women have these letters. It only means your prehistoric female ancestors most likely came from Europe, Central Asia, or the Middle East.

If your letters are A, B, C, D or X, most likely you could be Native American or Asian. The letter 'L" is African, and the letters M, A, B, C, D, E, F, G, O, P, Q and Z most likely are East Asian. A and C are shared with East Asian and Native American, and Z are found in Russia and Scandinavia at a low rate. These haplogroups are very ancient. Some are 20,000 or more than 50,000 years into prehistory. The letter X is found in Europe and among Native Americans, in the Middle East and in Central Asia.

If your mtDNA covers a wide area, it usually signifies that the DNA sequences are very ancient and had thousands of years to spread wide distances geographically. If your mtDNA sequences are found in a very narrow area, your mtDNA may have arisen relatively more recently. Your point of origin geographically is the place where your mtDNA is most diverse, not necessarily where it is found most frequently.

Where Can You Match YourmtDNA to a Country in an Online Database?

For women and men interested in matching their mtDNA sequences of HVS-1 or HVS-2 (high and low resolution) there are databases online such as Macaulay's Tables database. These DNA databases online are matched with surname groups, lists, message boards, and other Web and online databases to help you match your sequences to a geographic location. I use *Macaulay's Tables* at: http://www.stats.gla.ac.uk/~vincent/founder2000/tableA.html.

Roots for Real, based in London at: <http://www.rootsforreal.com/english/eng-home.html> tests your low resolution mtDNA or Y chromosome and sends you a report and map showing the probable or possible geographic origin of your sequence by latitude and longitude, even naming the town that exists there today. The probable geographic center for the origin of my mtDNA sequences is located at 48.30N, 4.65E, Bar sur Aube, France with a deviation of 669.62 miles according to the map emailed to me by Roots for Real.

Which Company to Choose and Why?

I had my DNA tested at Family Tree DNA, Oxford Ancestors, and Ancestry-ByDNA and geographical interpretations of the results done at Roots for Real. According to their Web site, Family Tree DNA coined the word anthrogenealogy "that combines the methods of the two sciences—anthropology and genealogy, "largely with individual or corporate sponsorship or carried out by avocational researchers."

Family Tree DNA gives a lot of choices. They sent me my sequences of both the high resolution and low resolution mtDNA called the HVS-1 and HVS-2. I was then able to look up on the Web "Macaulay's Tables," a database of sequences for HVS-1 and HVS-2 and find out in which countries people of today live who have my exact mtDNA sequences. The countries are England, Austria, Spain, and Bulgaria.

I chose to have my mtDNA interpreted by four companies so I could compare what they offered with what my goal was, to link genealogy to DNA and find out my matrilineal ancestry back to 21,000 years ago if that was possible as far as geographic location in longitude and latitude.

What I liked about each company was that they all offered different material. AncestryByDNA offered my genotype sequences on a CD and a racial percentages test. Oxford Ancestors offered a chart and a prehistory of the DNA that showed me how I link to the world's mtDNA clans. The company also showed me that 21,000 years ago my mtDNA lived in what was to become Spain and/or Southwest France.

The second company to test my mtDNA, *AncestryBy DNA* <http://www.ancestrybydna.com> in Sarasota, Florida, sent me a free book, titled, *The Great Human Diaspora*. It did help me understand how DNA is measured. For more information on the ancestry and migration of the male Y-chromosome, I found a newer book, *The Journey of Man*, by Spencer Wells, published in 2002.

Family Tree DNA tested my HVS-1 and HVS-2, my high and low resolution mtDNA. Roots for Real, London, sent me maps online that showed what latitude and longitude the probable origin of my exact mtDNA sequences appeared in the last 10,000 years and the town of probable origin that didn't exist in the distant past, the city of Bar Sur Aube, France.

What Will You Pay for a DNA Test for Ancestry?

In August 2001, Oxford Ancestors, London, became the first company to test my mtDNA for around $180. They noted my mtDNA sequences also showed up in England. They also sent me a chart showing where the mtDNA originated and how my mtDNA links with other mtDNA all over the world. I also received printed material on human migrations. I paid a little over $200 at Family Tree DNA. My husband paid $99 for a surname group-rate 12-marker Y-chromosome test at Family Tree DNA.

At most companies DNA tests can run from about $100 to over $300 for ancestry. Prices seem to be coming down and more markers are being tested for Y-chromosomes. DNA tests for nutrition or medical reasons are more, and a few companies even test the entire genome for a high price, more than $1,000.

How to Interpret DNA lineages—Males

Some DNA testing firms test 12, 25, or 37 markers of the male Y chromosome. The founder of your sequence might have originated around 10,000 years ago. To find the founder, DNA testing companies may work with university or private laboratories that test the Y-chromosome of males for ancestry. The laboratories test the Y chromosome of DNA for markers. Some of these markers are called short tandem repeats. These are, according to Spencer Wells in his book, *The Journey of Man*, "tandem repeats—short sections of the same sequence, repeated several times in a row in the DNA strand." Geneticists call them short tandem repeats.

Here's how you can do your own research independently of any laboratory that tested your own DNA if you're curious about Y-chromosome DNA tests. Males take Y-chromosome DNA tests to find out paternal ancestry lineages. Males also can have their mtDNA checked, but women don't have a Y chromosome. So women only can check their maternal lineages with mitochondrial (mtDNA) tests. According to Alastair Greenshields who runs Ybase at http://www.ybase.org, "Ybase is a free and open database which allows people to enter their Y-chromosome haplotype details independently of the laboratory they were tested at. Anyone can contribute to it and anyone can explore it."

The database can accept results for any of the 36 Y-chromosome markers currently in use along with other genealogical information. "Ybase is searchable for exact haplotype matches and/or near misses," says Greenshields. "Surnames, variant spellings and other relevant names can also be searched for, which is especially useful for the genealogist wishing to locate and contact others that share their sur-name and have had their DNA tested."

Most researchers that recognize their Y-chromosome cannot identify an actual individual and are happy to share their results online in an effort to find their DNA cousins and genetic roots. "Genealogical research coupled with DNA test-ing is already proving a very powerful method of substantiating ancestry," Green-shields explains. "And Ybase is sure to grow in line with this upward trend, benefiting the genealogical community as a whole."

Are male and female genetic lineages studied for different purposes? "Ybase is solely intended for Y-DNA and not mtDNA. A database of the latter would be so general and broad, given the nature of how mtDNA is passed on, as to be of little value to a researcher," Greenshields says.

Below are a couple of explanations on Y-DNA Alastair Greenshields wrote for two different people with entirely different backgrounds who needed the whole thing explained to them. "They explain essentially the same terms but have been 'dumbed down' to varying extents. Please feel entirely free to copy them verbatim or adjust as you deem necessary," says Greenshields.

To answer my question to Greenshields on how to interpret the results of DNA tests for Y-chromosome analysis for ancestry, he's explained it well in terms that most people can understand.

"Imagine a very long rope, some of which is lying across your desk. This is the DNA strand," Greenshields says. "It just happens to be the length of rope called 'Your Y-chromosome'.

"Now look at the bit that lies across your desk and grasp the rope with both hands, about half a meter apart. This is a 'marker' or 'locus' (Latin for 'place'). We'll call it DYS19.

"In between your hands, imagine that bit of rope is divided into 14 equally-spaced segments. If you look very closely at the segments, you can see that each one has a bit of writing on it, which reads TAGA.

"This is simply the DNA code for each repeat. Therefore the marker DYS19 = 14 repeats. Or if I ask you, 'What allele have you got for DYS19?' You can tell me '14'. (Allele effectively means the number of repeats.) For example, DYS19 has about nine possibilities (between 11 and 19).

"If you do the same at lots of different markers or loci (plural of locus), you'll get a whole series of numbers (DYS19=14, DYS388=15, DYS461=11 etc.). This is your 'haplotype'. It doesn't matter whether it is 20 or 200 numbers in length. This series of numbers is still called your haplotype.

"Now you are going to make some rope for your new son. You are pretty good at making rope and usually you can copy your own precisely, but this time you made it slightly too short. There are now 13 repeats. (Technically this is called a 'mutation' which can occur when an enzyme mis-types the DNA code). It still works perfectly well so your son keeps it and is very happy! There, you have it—DNA in a nutshell! (Be aware that your repeats, like the stock-market, may go up as well as down, but for entirely different reasons.)

Genealogy and the Y Chromosome

"DNA for the use of genealogy usually requires an analysis of your Y-chromosome," Greenshields explains. "Only males have this particular chromosome and the DNA code held within it is passed down from father to son (virtually) unchanged. Provided there is an unbroken paternal line between two males, that is both share a g-g-g-g-g-grandfather, their Y-chromosome DNA will be the same."

When the DNA is analyzed, many small sections are looked at. Presently, the testing companies look for anywhere between 10 and 26 sections or 'markers.' "At any one of the markers, the code will repeat itself, for example, 15 times," Greenshields explains. "If the marker is called DYS19, we can give the result DYS19 = 15."

If you analyze several of these markers, you end up with a 'haplotype'.

Thus you can compare haplotypes to see if you are related. "I say 'virtually' unchanged, as the DNA can change slightly over time due to 'mutations'—small errors formed when the DNA is copied," says Greenshields.

"When comparing the haplotypes from two people, this will show up as a 'mismatch'—where, for example, DYS 19 = 14."

These mutations are useful by themselves and occur at a fairly steady rate over time. "It also gives us the great variability that we observe over populations," says Greenshields.

"If the mutations did not occur, every male would have identical Y-chromosomes. Also, within DNA/genealogy studies, if many mismatches occur when comparing two male haplotypes, we can say that they are not related."

So you can see, DNA can be a very useful tool when comparing 'suspected' relatives. "But there is one caveat, however," Greenshields emphasizes. "You must share a surname, or have a very good reason to believe you are related. DNA alone will not identify your relatives from any other random person."

For example, you will probably share the same haplotype to at least someone in your home-town, but having a similar or same surname will raise the probabilities significantly. "DNA is a tool that should be overlaid on the existing genealogical records," notes Greenshield. "It can be an excellent way of deciding on further avenues of research, or indeed defining that there are several distinct lines within your family name."

What Information Can You Expect from DNA Testing Companies?

Oxford Ancestors <http://www.oxfordancestors.com> sent me a history of each of the 'clans' or haplogroups of my matrilineal DNA and a chart showing how my first female ancient ancestor who started the H mtDNA haplogroup linked to all the other world clans going back to the first anatomically modern human in Africa.

Next I went to Family Tree DNA. Their Web site is at: <http://www.familytreedna.com>. Soon Family Tree as well as AncestryByDNA offered the racial percentages test as well as the high and low resolution mtDNA testing. As time passes, more companies offer to test more Y-chromosome markers. Only men carry the Y-chromosome.

What I like about Family Tree DNA are the choices. You can test males for a variety of number of Y-chromosome markers such as 12, 25, or more. They have surname projects and various ethnic databases. There's a Jewish database, for example, that is linked to various research projects. There are tests for Native American DNA

Where Can You Match YourmtDNA to a Country in an Online Database?

For women and men interested in matching their mtDNA sequences of HVS-1 or HVS-2 (high and low resolution) there are databases online such as Macaulay's Tables Database. These DNA databases online are matched with surname groups, lists, message boards, and other Web and online databases to help you match your sequences to a geographic location. I use *Macaulay's Tables* at: http://www.stats.gla.ac.uk/~vincent/founder2000/tableA.html

What you can expect from a DNA test is to use molecular genetics to observe your DNA data trail of a lineage. The test results allow you to use genealogy and

DNA test results together to connect unknown family members by locations on non-Recombining Y or mtDNA markers. You inherit your Y chromosome or mtDNA from your father and mother. It's the same markers that show up in your great grand parents all the way back to the first ancestor of your sequences that appeared 10,000 or 20,000 years ago depending on your sequences.

Should Genealogists Learn Anthrogenealogy?

Anthrogenealogy is Family Tree DNA's word of choice "for the study of deep genealogical origins through means of genetics." From AncestryByDNA, the third company that tested my DNA, I received a package containing a map of the world with the theory of how humans evolved from Africa to the rest of the world. The map showed that traces of these ancient African markers or genes are found in all people today. The fourth company I contacted, Roots for Real, asked for the results of my mtDNA tests at the other DNA companies.

Roots for Real is a London-based DNA testing company that presently tests your HVS-1, low-resolution MtDNA sequences. The company asked for the results of my mtDNA test from any other DNA testing company. I sent them my sequences. What I like about Roots for Real is that they emailed me the possible geographic center of origin on the map and a list of my mtDNA matches by geographic coordinates. This consisted of a list of how many people tested are living in various countries. It's a guess made from computing the center of the geographic area, because there's a deviation or migration from that theoretical center of 669.62 miles, and that center turns up in France, even though people with my sequence now live within a radius of 669.62 miles of that center.

No people's names were mentioned on the list or database, only code numbers, the country, and how many tested were living in that country at the time of the study. The geographic center of possible origin on the map Roots for Real sent me is 48.30N 4.65E, Bar sur Aube, France with a deviation of 669.62 miles. For further information, their Web site is at: <http://www.rootsforreal.com>. You can write to Roots for Real at: PO Box 43708, London W14 8WG UK.

6

Ashkenazim and Eastern Europeans: Mediterranean Markers in Poland

If you want to get at the roots of your ancestry through studies in population genetics, read the article that will take you back before there were borders or organized religions titled, "*Tracing European Founder Lineages in the Near Eastern mtDNA Pool.*" Martin Richards, Vincent Macaulay, et al. American Journal of Human Genetics, 67: 1251–1276, 2000. See where our mothers really came from. (The term "our mothers" refers to the human race.)

You'll notice in the articles you read that the British often use the term "Near Eastern" and that the Americans use the term "Middle Eastern" for the same area. Make time capsules of your DNA information for future generations to look back at their ancestor's medical histories and genetic data. Put in explanations of how to interpret your tests and printouts or reports.

Perhaps you want to find out the percentage of various races in your ancestry. How do know where to begin your journey into the past and future? What if you're a foundling, an orphan, or have no knowledge of your own ethnicity? Can a DNA test at least tell you how many races are in your recent or ancient past? What facts do genetic markers really tell you about ancestry?

If you want to start your ancestry search with DNA testing, first you take the DNA tests along with tests of racial percentages if you desire. Even your DNA has a cultural component to its molecular biology. Then you interpret the results making the complex easy to understand for yourself or your clients. Your DNA testing service can help you find answers. So can many Web sites as well as this book and other books recommended here.

Next in your family history search, you collect letters, diaries, oral history transcriptions, home sources, artifacts, memorabilia, Census research, wills-and-probate records, medical histories, land records, slave ownership records, if it applies to your or your client. Pay particular attention to social histories to fill some gaps left by lack of women's records.

Search through church, synagogue, mosque, pagoda, or temple records, vital records from the US government such as military records, social security information, and government pensions for retired government employees, employment and tax records, if any exist and are available. Check school records from elementary through college, if any, social histories, ethnic histories, and religious school records.

Go to the family history Web sites, the ships' passenger lists. I highly recommend a book for searching women's ancestry, titled, Discovering Your Female Ancestors, by Sharon DeBartolo Carmack, Betterway Books, Ohio 1998, ISBN # 1-55870-472-8. The book's subtitle emphasizes "Special strategies for uncovering hard-to-find information about your female lineage."

Marriage records often were in different languages representing the former country or languages of the ethnic group. You may need to translate a different alphabet to find a maiden name on a marriage certificate never registered, but obtained from clergy.

Then you review and analyze the records. Study the social history of the times and location of this individual. Add family history and migrations to social history, and you have the beginnings of an outline to write a biography of the ancestor as a family history.

Learn to interpret the results of your own DNA test and expand your historical research ability to trace your ancestry. "An interesting idea was expressed by a colleague from Canada, Dr. Charles Scriver," explains geneticist, Dr. Batsheva Bonné-Temir. "At a meeting which I organized here in Israel on Genetic Diversity Among Jews in 1990, Dr. Scriver gave a paper on 'What Are Genes Like that Doing in a Place Like This?

Human History and Molecular Prosopography.'

"He claimed that a biological trait has two histories, a biological component and a cultural component." Dr. Charles Scriver is founder of the DeBelle Laboratory of Biochemical Genetics in Canada. He also established screening programs in Montreal for thalassaemia and Tay Sachs Disease."

According to Bonné-Tamir, at the 1990 meeting in Israel on Genetic Diversity Among Jews, Dr. Charles Scriver stated, "When the event clusters and an important cause of it is biological, the cultural history also is likely to be important because it may explain why the persons carrying the gene are in the particular place at the time."

The term, "when the event clusters" refers to an event when genes cluster together in a DNA test because the genes are similar in origin, that is, they have a common ancestral origin in a particular area, a common ancestor.

"When I look at my own papers throughout the years," says Bonné-Tamir. "I find that I have been quite a pioneer in realizing the significance of combining the history of individuals or of populations with their biological attributes. This is now a leading undertaking in many studies which use, for example, mutations to estimate time to the most recent ancestors and alike."

What lines of inquiry are used in genetics? Dr. Charles R. Scriver wrote a chapter in Batsheva Bonné-Temir's book, titled What are genes like that doing in a place like this? Human History and Molecular Prosopography. The book title is: Genetic Diversity Among Jews: Diseases and Markers at the DNA Level. Bonné-Tamir, B. and Adam, A. Oxford University Press. 1992.

With permission, an excerpt is reprinted below from page 319: "When a disease clusters in a particular community, two lines of inquiry follow:

1.   Is the clustering caused by shared environmental exposure? Or is it explained by host susceptibility accountable to biological and/or cultural inheritance?

2.   If the explanation is biological, how are the determinants inherited? These lines of inquiry imply that a disease has two different histories, one biological, the other cultural. One involves genes (heredity), pathways of development (ontogeny), and constitutional factors; the other, demography, migration and cultural practice.

Neither history is mutually exclusive. Such thinking shifts the focus of inquiry from sick populations and incidence of disease to sick individuals and the cause of their particular disease. The person with the disease becomes the object of concern which is not the same as the disease the person has." (Page. 319).

After hearing from Dr. Scriver by email, I then emailed Stanley M. Diamond. He contacted writer, Barbara Khait, and got permission for me to reprint in this book some of what she wrote about Diamond's project. It's the chapter, "Genetics Study Identifies At-risk relatives" from **Celebrating the Family** published by Ancestry.com Publishing. Check out the Web site at: http://shops.ancestry.com/product.asp?productid=2625&shopid=128.

Here's the reprinted article. Persons interested may go to the Web site for more information. I found out about Stanley M. Diamond from Dr. Scriver, since he mentioned Stanley M. Diamond's project in the book chapter Scriver wrote for Batsheva Bonné-Temir's book on *Genetic Diversity Among Jews: Diseases and Markers at the DNA Level.* Barbara Khait's chapter follows.

"In 1977, Stanley Diamond of Montreal learned he carried the betathalassemia genetic trait. Though common among people of Mediterranean, Middle Eastern, Southeast Asian and African descent, the trait is rare among descendants of eastern European Jews like Stan. His doctor made a full study of the family and identified Stanley's father as the source.

"Stan was spurred to action by a letter his brother received in 1991 from a previously unknown first cousin. Stan asked the cousin, "Do you carry the beta-thalassemia trait?" Though the answer was no, Stan began his journey to find out what other members of his family might be unsuspecting carriers.

"Later that year, Stan found a relative from his paternal grandmother's family, the Widelitz family. Again he asked, "Is there any incidence of anemia in your family?" His newfound cousin answered, "Oh, you mean beta-thalassemia? It's all over the family!"

"There was no question now that the trait could now be traced to Stan's grandmother, Masha Widelitz Diamond and that Masha's older brother Aaron also had to have been a carrier. Stan's next question: who passed the trait onto Masha and Aaron? Was it their mother, Sura Nowes, or their father, Jankiel Widelec?

"At the 1992 annual summer seminar on Jewish genealogy in New York City, Stan conferred with Dr. Robert Desnick, who suggested that Stan's first step should be to determine whether the trait was related to a known mutation or a gene unique to his family. He advised Stan to seek out another Montrealer, Dr. Charles Scriver of McGill University-Montreal Children's Hospital. With the help of a grant, Dr. Scriver undertook the necessary DNA screening with the goal of determining the beta-thalassemia mutation.

"During this time, Stan began to research his family's history in earnest and identified their nineteenth century home town of Ostrow Mazowiecka in Poland. **With the help of birth, marriage, and death records for the Jewish population of Ostrow Mazowiecka filmed by The Church of Jesus Christ of Latter-day Saints (LOS), Stan was able to construct his family tree.**

"Late in 1993, Dr. Scriver faxed the news that the mutation had been identified and that it was, in fact, a novel mutation. Independently, Dr. Ariella Oppenheim at Jerusalem's Hebrew University-Hadassah Hospital mad e a similar discovery about a woman who had recently emigrated from the former Soviet Union.

"The likelihood that we were witnessing a DNA region 'identical by descent' in the two families was impressive. We had apparently discovered a familial relationship between Stanley and the woman in Jerusalem, previously unknown to either family," says Dr. Scriver.

"It wasn't very long ago when children born with thalassemia major seldom made it past the age of ten. Recent advances have increased life span but, to stay alive, these children must undergo blood transfusions every two to four weeks. And every night, they must receive painful transfusions of a special drug for up to twelve hours.

"The repeated blood transfusions lead to a buildup of iron in the body that can damage the heart, liver, and other organs. That's why, when the disease is misdiagnosed as mild chronic anemia, the prescription of additional iron is even more harmful. Right now, no cure exists for the disease, though medical experts say experimental bone-marrow transplants and gene-therapy procedures may one day lead to one.

"Stan's primary concern is that carriers of thalassemia trait may marry, often unaware that their mild chronic anemia may be something else. To aid in his search for carriers of his family's gene mutation of the beta-thalassemia trait, he founded and coordinates an initiative known as Jewish Records Indexing-Poland, an award-winning Internet-based index of Jewish vital records in Poland, with more than one million references. This database is helping Jewish families, particularly those at increased risk for hereditary conditions and diseases, trace their medical histories, as well as geneticists."

Says Dr. Robert Burk, professor of epidemiology at the Albert Einstein College of Medicine at Yeshiva University, and principal investigator for the Cancer Longevity, Ancestry and Lifestyle (CLAL) study in the Jewish population (currently focusing on prostate cancer), "Through the establishment of a searchable database from Poland, careful analysis of the relationship between individuals will be possible at both the familial and the molecular level.

"This will afford us the opportunity to learn not only more about the Creator's great work, but will also allow (us) researchers new opportunities to dissect the cause of many diseases in large established pedigrees."

Several other medical institutions, including Yale University's Cancer Genetics Program, the Epidemiology-Genetics Program at the Johns Hopkins School of Medicine, and Mount Sinai Hospital's School of Medicine have recognized Diamond's work as an outstanding application of knowing one's family history and as a guide to others who may be trying to trace their medical histories, particularly those at increased risk for hereditary conditions and diseases.

In February 1998, in a breakthrough effort, Stanley discovered another member of his family who carried the trait. He found the descendants of Jankiel's niece and nephew—first cousins who married—David Lustig and his wife, Fanny Bengelsdorf. This was no ordinary find—he located the graves by **using a map of the Ostrow Mazowiecka section of Chicago's Waldheim Cemetery** and contacted the person listed as the one paying for perpetual care, David and Fanny's grandson, Alex.

"It turned out Alex, too, had been diagnosed as a beta-thalassemia carrier by his personal physician fifteen years earlier. The discovery that David and Fanny's descendants were carriers of the beta-thalassemia trait convinced Stan, Dr. Scriver, and Dr.Oppenheim that Hersz Widelec, **born in 1785**, must be the source of the family's novel mutation.

'This groundbreaking work helps geneticists all over the world understand the trait and its effects on one family,' says Dr. Oppenheim.

"A most important contribution of Stanley Diamond's work is increasing the awareness among his relatives and others to the possibility that they carry a genetic trait which with proper measures, can be prevented in future generations. In addition, the work has demonstrated the power of modern genetics in identifying distant relatives, and helps to clarify how genetic diseases are being spread throughout the world."

For more information about thalassemia, contact Cooley's Anemia Foundation (129-09 26th Avenue. Flushing, New York, 11354; by phone 800-522-7222; or online at www.cooleysanemia.org). For more about Stanley Diamond's research. visit his Web site (www.diamondgen.org).

Thalassemia is not only carried by people living today in Mediterranean lands. The first Polish (not Jewish) carrier of Beta-Thal was discovered in the last few years in Bialystok, Poland. Stanley Diamond met with the Director of the Hematology Institute in Warsaw in November 2002, and the Director of the Hematology Institute in Warsaw indicated that they now have identified 52 carriers. Check out these Web sites listed below if the subject intrigues you.

"Genealogy with an extra reason"...Beta-Thalassemia Research Project.
http://www.diamondgen.org
JTA genetic disorder and Polish Jewish history
www.jta.org/page_view_story.asp?intarticleid=11608&intcategoryid=5
IAJGS Lifetime Achievement Award
http://www.jewishgen.org/ajgs/awards.html

Jewish Records Indexing—Poland
http://www.jri-poland.org

Geneticists today are making inroads in new areas such as phenomics, nutritional genomics, and ancestral genetics. Batsheva Bonné-Tamir, PhD, http://www.tau.ac.il/medicine/USR/bonnétamirb.htm or http://www.tau.ac.il/medicine/ at Tel-Aviv University, Israel, is Head of the National Laboratory for the Genetics of Israeli Populations (with Mia Horowitz) and Director of the Shalom and Varda Yoran Institute for Genome Research Tel-Aviv. She is also on the faculty of the Department of Human Genetics and Molecular Medicine, Sackler School of Medicine.

Dr. Bonné-Tamir states that "One of my most impressive conclusions from the advancement in the last few years and the accumulation of knowledge in the fields of genetics and medicine, is the molecular revolution based on immense sophistication of lab techniques. This is really responsible for the recent increased emphasis on the human-social-anthropological aspects that affect biological diversity."

Bonné-Tamir explains, "At a meeting in 1973, in my paper on Merits and Difficulties in Studies of Middle Eastern Isolates, I said that 'The Middle Eastern isolates have emphasized again the fertile and necessary interrelationship between history and genetics.'"

Do historical events influence genes? "Comparative studies in population genetics are often undertaken in order to attempt reconstruction of historical and migratory movements based on gene frequencies," says Bonné-Tamir. "The Samaritans and Karaites offer opportunities in the opposite direction, for example, to learn the influence of historical events on gene frequencies."

In another paper in 1979 on Analysis of Genetic Data on Jewish Populations, Dr. Bonné-Temir wrote that "Our purpose in studying the differences and similarities between various Jewish populations was not to determine whether a Jewish race exists. Nor was it to discover the original genes of 'ancient Hebrews,' or to retrieve genetic characteristics in the historical development of the Jews.

"Rather, it was to evaluate the extent of 'heterogeneity' in the separate opulations, to construct a profile of each population as shaped by the genetic data, and to draw inferences about the possible influences of dispersion, migration, and admixture processes on the genetic composition of these populations."

In 1999, Dr. Bonné-Temir organized an international symposium on Genomic Views of Jewish History. "And unfortunately, the many papers presented were never published," says Bonné-Temir.

Molecular Genealogy Research Projects

Certain mtDNA haplogroups and mutations or markers within the haplogroups turn up in research studies of Ashkenazim when scientists look at the maternal lineages. For example, 9.0 of Ashkenazic (Jewish) women have mtDNA haplogroups that follow the Cambridge Reference Sequence (CRS) (Anderson et al. 1981).

That means their matrilineal ancestry lines follow the reference sequence that all other mtDNA haplogroup markers are compared with. The CRS shows a specific sequence of mtDNA haplogroup H found in more than 46% of all Europeans and 6% of Middle Eastern peoples. Note that H haplogroup mtDNA in general with various mutations shows up in about 25% of Middle Eastern peoples, but only 6% of Middle Eastern peoples have mtDNA H haplogroup that exactly follows the Cambridge Reference Sequence (CRS).

You can view a table of mtDNA sequences titled "Frequently Encountered mtDNA Hapotypes" at Table 3 in the article, "*Founding Mothers of Jewish Communities: Geographically Separated Jewish Groups Were Independently Founded by Very Few Female Ancestors,*" Mark G. Thomas et al, American Journal of Human Genetics, 70:1411–1420, 2002.

The only exception is that the Ashkenazic mtDNA haplogroup maternal ancestral lines, show up at only 2.6% with one mutation away from the CRS 343 creating U3 mtDNA haplogroup instead of the H mtDNA haplogroup. The CRS is H haplogroup. Where does U3 mtDNA show up at the higher rate of 17%? In Iraqi Jews. Ashkenazi mtDNA shows up at 9.0 percent following the CRS with H mtDNA haplogroup.

Yet 27.0% of Moroccan Jews have mtDNA following the CRS. So do more than 46% of all Europeans. That's haplogroup H of the Cambridge Reference Sequence.

The table in the article mentioned above has many sequences of mtDNA listed. Ashkenazi mtDNA was compared to MtDNA in other Jewish groups—Moroccan, Iraqi, Iranian, Georgian, Bukharan, Yemenite, Ethopian, and Indian. These were compared to non-Jewish Germans, Berbers, Syrians, Georgian non-Jews, Uzbeks, Yemenites, Ethiopian non-Jews, Hindus, and Israeli Arabs. The percentage of frequencies of HSV-1 mtDNA sequences were listed in the samples from sites 16090–16365.

Looking only at Ashkenazi mtDNA, the mutations 184 and 265T show up in 2.6% of the Ashkenazi mtDNA. Yet in Jews from Bukhara, these same mutations show up in 15.2% of mtDNA.

And 129 and 223 mutations show up in 2.6% of the Ashkenazi mtDNA. Yet in Bukharian Jewish mtDNA, this mutation shows up at 12.1%. The rest of the Ashkenazi mtDNA stands at 9.0% for matching the CRS. That's H haplogroup, the most frequent mtDNA haplogroup found in Europe. Only 1.3% of Ashkenazic mtDNA has one mutation at 274. Yet 20% of Yemenite Jewish mtDNA shows this same mutation at 274.

Be aware that not every Jewish person has been tested for mtDNA or Y-chromosomes. You first have to research how significant samples are in speaking for the majority of any population. They do have scientific credibility, but you must always look at the sample size.

Men carry their mother's mtDNA but pass on to their sons their Y-chromosome. Women pass on their mtDNA haplogroup only to their daughters.

Genomic views of any ethnic group's history are important for further study. Whether you are taking the skeptic's position or the genomic view of your cultural history, biology does have a cultural component that needs to be analyzed scientifically. Finding flaws or benefits in research studies of any kind is the way to find inroads to truths. How else can facts change and knowledge progress?

Molecular genealogy has joined efforts with molecular genetics. The Sorenson Molecular Genealogy Foundation (SMGF) is a nonprofit organization that was founded to build a correlated genetic and genealogical database. How can this information help you in family history research? Ugo A. Perego, MS. Senior Project Administrator, Molecular Genealogy Research Project, Brigham Young University, http://molecular-genealogy.byu.edu , and now with the Sorenson Molecular Genealogy Foundation at: http://www.smgf.org/ says, "I believe that DNA is the next thing in genealogy—the tool for the 21st century family historians.

In the past 20 years, the genealogical world has been revolutionized by the introduction of the Internet.

"An increasing number of people are becoming interested in searching for their ancestors because through emails and websites a large world of family history information is now available to them. The greatest contribution of molecular methods to family history is the fact that in some instances family relationships and blocked genealogies can be extended even in the absence of written records.

"Adoptions, illegitimacies, names that have been changes, migrations, wars, fire, flood, etc. are all situations in which a record may become unavailable. However, no one can change our genetic composition, which we have received by those that came before us.

"Currently, DNA testing is an effective approach to help with strict paternal and maternal lines thanks to the analysis and comparison of the Y chromosome (male line) and mitochondrial DNA (female line) in individuals that have reason to believe the existence of a common paternal or maternal ancestor.

"A large database of genetic and genealogical data is currently been built by the BYU Center for Molecular Genealogy and the Sorenson Molecular Genealogy Foundation. This database will contain thousands of pedigree charts and DNA from people from all over the world. Currently it has already over 35,000 participants in it.

"The purpose of this database is to provide additional knowledge in reconstructing family lines other than the paternal and maternal, by using a large number of autosomal DNA (the DNA found in the non-sex chromosomes).

This research, known as the Molecular Genealogy Research Project is destined to take DNA for genealogists to the next level." For additional reading, please visit the BYU's Molecular Genealogy Research Project's two Web sites. Another good source of information is at http://www.relativegenetics.com, a company specialized in Y chromosome analysis for family studies.

For further information about the Sorenson Molecular Genealogy Foundation, contact them at the following address:

Sorenson Molecular Genealogy Foundation
2511 South West Temple
Salt Lake City, UT 84115

Phone: (801) 461-9780
After hours phone: (801) 244-2542
Fax: (801) 461-9761
Email: info@smgf.org

7

Family Histories as Evidence of Who We Are

Family stories are *evidence* of who we are. 'Salable' life stories usually are launched in the media—the major national press of credible repute—before they are produced as a video or movie and published as a book. Personal histories, like corporate histories may end up as time capsules on disk and on Web sites as video and audio documentaries or in books.

Time capsules may contain personal histories, corporate histories, and even DNA-driven genealogy reports along with keepsake memorabilia. Material is documented on video, audio, and in text format. It's truly a multimedia production. Oral history tapes are transcribed and archived in libraries and museums. Here's how to document your personal history and launch a salable life story.

Write and produce as a video or audio your personal or oral history. Or present a folkloric tradition. Your salable life story can be presented as a time capsule, disk, Web site and keepsake album. The format may be a dramatic script, book, article, story, skit, radio broadcast, diary, novel, letter, article, monologue, or poem.

Cut and paste the text file into synthetic voice software and have it read and saved in your computer in most languages or with selected male or female voices or regional accents. Then 'burn' it to a DVD, CD, or any other format. Your life story is now saved in multimedia as a time capsule.

Before you think about publishing your life story or anyone else's, launch the personal history in the media. If you are working with someone else's life story, you'll need a signed release form allowing you to put the story on your Web site and/or on disk.

Be sure your form releases you from liability resulting from someone else's name going public for educational and scholarly research. Start with your own personal history and learn what pitfalls to avoid. Gain insight, foresight, and hindsight.

Personal and oral history taping and archiving also branches into fields such as folklore and oral tradition, anthropology and ethnology. A personal historian can be an employee or an independent contractor. You can transcribe oral history tapes or work with creating audio and video files from your already written book or story.

So You Want to Be a Personal Historian or Video Biographer

So you want to be a personal historian? You are worth the storage. Launch your own personal history business by first doing a personal history on yourself and members of your family. You can include corporate histories, success story case histories, and life story writing circles for individuals. When somebody asks you for the facts, the primary source for research on your life story, only you can supply the evidence. This evidence is valuable. It's all about who you are, what you stand for, and how you reached out to others.

Showcase your own life history for your family, friends, or historians. Your life story is valuable now and in the distant future. You are part of history. Make sure a release form goes into your time capsule with your multimedia wishes concerning your life story in any format.

Maybe you'd also like to make time capsules? What about including DNA-driven genealogy reports as keepsake memorabilia? Include life stories, genealogy records, oral traditions, and folkloric customs. What's more valuable than a life story? You can focus on intergenerational writing, autobiographies, diaries, journals, video biographies, oral histories, corporate histories, tales, oral history tape transcribing. Or concentrate on life story writing in the form of books, video, audio, Web sites, skits, poems, memoirs, creative writing, greeting card CDs, DVD and video productions. Transfer tapes to disk. Design Web video broadcasting or make time capsules.

Write your own personal history. How do you write and launch salable life stories in the media, in the publishing world, and in the world of video, multimedia, Internet multicasting, Web-based historical documentaries, life-story-based novels, and film?

Every life story has four seasons and twelve stages like the months in a year. The four seasons are infancy, childhood, adulthood, and grace-age. Or you want to be an oral traditionalist, folklorist, or oral historian, folklore librarian, or archivist and conservator of old videos, photos, letters, articles, disks, and books. What makes your personal history salable? Marketability is born in the national media. Credible journalism launches your story to agents, entertainment attorneys, publishers and producers long before your book is published or your video is made available to the public through your Web site, DVD, CD greeting card, or other time capsule.

Maybe you want to know how to promote and publicize life stories in the media before they are published as books or produced cinematically. Or you want to write, promote, and sell your autobiography—commercially—to a selected niche market audience.

Personal histories are found in books, video, film, audio, and games. Depending upon your field of focus, your autobiography or anyone else's life story can become a salable personal history. A life story becomes 'commercial' or salable when it is launched in the national press before it is published as a book or produced as a movie or video.

It also can become a time capsule on disk and/or on an Internet Web site. An audio or video tape on the Web is part of a personal broadcasting network. Personal and corporate histories are time capsules. Oral histories may be transcribed into text.

Text writings may be imported or cut and pasted into synthetic voice software and quickly turned into audio files, DVDs, CDs, or tapes and uploaded to a Web site to be broadcast much like a personal radio station or broadcasting network. Audio or video files can be uploaded to Web sites and download to personal computers anywhere in the world with Internet access. The files can be saved by right-clicking a computer mouse and "saved as a target" in anyone's computer and then played on a computer hard disk drive or saved to other disks or transferred to tapes or DVDs or CDs or most any other media.

Live voices or synthetic software voices can read text and be saved as a computer file much the same as any audio or video file. And to make sure text stays as readable text, books of all sizes or skits and plays or scripts can be written or transcribed from oral interviews of anyone's life story. The same may be done for the oral history of a corporation, or for folklore tradition.

It's all part of a career as a personal and/or oral historian. Here, anthropology, history, ethnology, creative writing, genealogy, and public speaking combine. You can even put printouts and reports of DNA-driven genealogy research on a person or family in a genealogy-related time capsule to be opened by future generations.

In the time capsule could be video and audio material, text writings, diaries, oral traditions, and anything related to life story writing. Keepsakes and poetry, dramatizations, skits, plays, and the reminiscing of individuals, groups, or corporations may go into a time capsule. What used to be keepsake albums (scrapbooks) can now become time capsules.

If you want to be a personal historian, you can open an independent business where you travel in an area in order to 'videotape' people with your camcorder, usually in digital high 8 format, and transcribe the tapes to appear as text transcripts of what they said orally on the video or audio tape, CD, or DVD.

You can spend up to six hours transcribing a one-hour video or audio tape. Often there are two voices, the interviewer and the interviewee on the tape. Some people may want to speak into a tape recorder or camcorder and tape themselves when they are alone in a room without an interviewer. These people would receive a list of questions to look at so they can answer focusing on turning points or highlight the significant events in their lives.

You may want to tape a group of people speaking for five to seven minutes each on a special topic such as what did you do during World War II? Maybe the people in the group would describe what it was like living in a certain place during a certain decade or working in a certain environment or occupation.

Life story tapes usually run about an hour for individuals to talk about their entire life history in five minute segments. Fifteen five-minute segments can bring them up to age seventy-five. These can be taped weekly or daily during a fifteen-week 'semester' or fifteen days of daily taping where they speak in five-minute 'chunks' on one videotape. The five minute segments allows art work, photos, slides, or video clips of other scenes, such as the house they live in or anything pertinent to be taped or photographed and edited in between segments. A personal history taping can run as a 15-week class in life story writing. For those who don't want to appear on camera, audio tape can be used in a tape recorder.

Most people find it difficult to sit in front of a camcorder for one hour and continuously speak or answer questions. Some enjoy an interview that does last an hour. Others would rather use the five-minute segments and have you tape them in a classroom setting or their home another day, perhaps each day at the same time during a 15-week 'semester.'

Personal history may be done as an adult education course in any type of setting from recreation room of an assisted living facility or senior community center to a private home or public classroom in an adult education class in life story writing. If you're running a class, you might have the people meet from 11 am to noon each Sunday, perhaps right after their 10 am church service for a taping.

Each person can spend as much time as he or she wants—either one five-minute segment or perhaps three segments totaling fifteen minutes each week until the one-hour tape is completed. You can include, if desired, a DNA-driven genealogy report in case the person wants a DNA test for ancestry to put into a time capsule for family members and future generations. The time capsule would contain a text version of the life story of each member of the family or of one individual. It would also have a video tape, an audio tape, any keepsakes, and the creative work such as poetry or skits and writings or art work, photos, and other memorabilia that can fit into the time capsule.

A video or audio tape would also be preserved on a DVD and a CD, and if possible, uploaded to a Web site as a video and/or audio file of the individual or one of the family members who has access to the Internet and can purchase Web site space allowing a video and audio file to be uploaded along with the text transcription or life story writing of the individual. This makes a wonderful time capsule gift in personal history.

You'll want to know how to write it so that it can be marketed to your niche customers or audience. Maybe you'll combine your personal history with a practical invention of some type, such as an inexpensive device everyone can use or a special cooking utensil. This book is about becoming a personal historian. From there, your works can diverge into many roads or branches that link back to personal history.

Why do you want to write a personal history of someone or an autobiography of yourself and make it commercial to sell to a niche or wide audience? You may want to flummox the readers and enhance their public or private lives. You may want to protect an institution from mockery. Or you want to take a stand and speak in codes that are the shorthand of living.

To be concrete, writing and/or producing or transcribing personal history, oral history, folklore and oral tradition may focus on taking a stand on specific areas of life such as recording your experience being bullied in elementary school and focusing on taking a stand by writing a series of teaching guides with a training videotape or disk featuring your personal history and the personal histories of others with similar past experiences.

Maybe you want to join your personal history with others' personal histories in a documentary disk or tape defending a symbol of religious or ethnic identity. Should you wear that symbol in public, for example, in school or at work or during travel? Should you defend that symbol with a time capsule, an oral history, or personal history videotape, DVD, and text material? On your Web site in multimedia? In a keepsake album?

In what do you seek comfort? Your personal history can be about seeking comfort in food, work, play, care giving, leisure, travel, research, art, writing, or whatever you choose. What's your crusade about and how would you describe or show your slogan?

If you write a commercial autobiography, you'll want to know how to market your work. You might wish to make time capsules to preserve the highlights of life stories of older adults or corporations. You can carve out a career as a personal historian and interview people, record what they say on a variety of media, and have the tapes transcribed to text or transcribe them yourself. You can conserve paper or videos, transfer the medium to new technologies such as video tape to DVD disks, or make keepsake albums and multimedia time capsules. 'Scrap booking' can become oral tradition or personal history.

What you're creating are keepsakes or time capsules. And what is a keepsake to the average person becomes a time capsule to an oral historian and archaeologist. You can even include DNA-driven genealogy reports in a keepsake or time capsule.

Maybe you want to write commercial biographies or your autobiography. Perhaps you'll ghostwrite other people's autobiographies. Or you'll perhaps choose to write corporate biographies and success stories and be a case history manager or consultant for new companies. You can transcribe oral histories. Another route is to produce or tape video biographies and archive them in oral history libraries, usually at universities, museums, or other foundations.

8

What Makes a Personal History, Genealogy as Creative Non-Fiction, or Life Story Salable?

Also: **How to Transcribe Oral Histories: Alternative Career for Historians, Genealogists, Anthropologists, and Freelance Writers**

Q. What makes a life story saleable?
A. Buzz appeal. High velocity personal memoir. A life story is salable when it has universal appeal and identity. An example is a single parent making great sacrifices to put bread on the table and raise a decent family in hard times. Many people identify with the universal theme of a life story. Buzz appeal draws in the deep interest of the press to publicize and lend credibility to a life story, to put a spin on it in the media, and to sell it to the public because all readers may be able to see themselves in your life story.

Q. To whom do you sell your life story to?
A. You sell your life story to publishers specializing in life stories. If you look under biographies in a book such as Writer's Guide to Book Editors, Publishers, and Literary Agents, 1999–2000, by Jeff Herman, Prima Publishing, you'll see several pages of publishers of life story, biography, and memoirs or autobiography. A few include The Anonymous Press, Andrews McMeel Publishing, Applause Theatre Book Publishers, Barricade Books, Inc., Baskerville Publishers, and many more listed in that directory. Also take a look at Writers Market, Writers Digest Books, checkout Memoirs in the index. Publishers include Feminist Press, Hachai, Hollis, Narwhal, Northeastern University Press, Puppy House, Westminster, John Knox,and others. Check categories such as creative nonfiction, biography, ethnic, historical, multicultural and other categories for lists of

publishers in your genre. Don't overlook writing your life story as a play, mono-logue, or script or for the audio book market.

Q. How do you present your life story in order to turn it into a saleable book, article, play, or other type of literature so that other people will want to read it?

A. You write a high-velocity powerful personal memoir or autonomedia which emphasizes cultural criticism and theory. Or you write a factual expose, keep a journal on the current cultural pulse, or write a diary about what it feels like to be single and dating in your age group—thirty something, sixty-something, or what-ever you choose. You become an investigative biographer. You write a riveting love story. Or how to use love to heal. Or you write about breaking through old barriers to create new publishing frontiers.

Q. How do you write a commercial biography?

A. Make sure someone wants to buy it before you write the whole thing. The details will be forthcoming in the course as it begins. Then contact the press, reporters in the media with credibility who write for a national daily newspaper or reputable magazine. Also contact radio and cable TV stations to do interviews on a selected event in your life story or biography. Pick a niche market where the particular audience has a special interest in that experience.

Q. The difference between authorized and unauthorized.

A. Authorized means you have permission and approval from the person about whom you're writing.

Q. Who gets assigned to write biographies of celebrities or other famous people?

A. Usually newspaper columnists who cover the beat or subject area, or you're a known writer who contacts an agent specializing in writing or ghostwriting celebrity biographies. You can enter this profession from many doors. I'll explain in the course.

Writing Your Ending First Gives You Closure And Clues How To Solve The Problems In Your Life Story. Teaching Life Story Writing On The Internet

When you write a salable life story, it's easier to write your ending first. Even-tually, with experience working with a variety of life stories, you can start quality circles or classes in life story writing (writing your salable memoirs, autobiography, biography, corporate history, family history, your diary as a commercial novel or play or true confession, true story, or true crime book or story or script).

Also, you can teach life story writing, interviewing, or videobiography on the Internet for yourself or for an existing school or program. It's relaxing and comforting to sit at home in perfect quiet and type a lecture into a screen browser such as the courses that can be offered through www.blackboard.com and other programs. Or teach online using a live chat screen. Customize your course to the needs of your students. You may need certification or a graduate degree to teach for a university online, but there's also adult education classes given in nontraditional settings such as churches, libraries, and museums.

Online, you can offer independent classes and go into business for yourself as a personal historian. Another way is to offer time capsules, keepsake albums, gift baskets, greeting cards, life stories on video, DVD, or transcribed from oral history. Work with libraries, museums, or your own independent classes. You can work at home or be mobile and travel to other people's homes or senior centers and assisted living recreation rooms, community centers, or schools and theaters to work with life stories.

Some companies have put life-story recording kiosks in public places such as train stations or airports. Check out the StoryCorps Web site at http://www. storycorps.net/. Find your own mission or purpose and create your own business recording the life stories of a variety of people in video, sound, text, or multimedia formats. It's all part of the time-capsule generation that emphasizes your life story has value and needs to be preserved as part of history. The revelation is that your life story isn't only for your family and friends anymore. As part of history, the world can now experience the one universal that connects us—life, and within a life story—insight, foresight, and hindsight.

Diaries of senior citizens are in demand. To sell them, you need buzz appeal, visibility in the press for writing simple stories of how you struggled to put bread on the table and raised a family alone, or what you've learned from your mistakes or experiences, how you solved problems, gave yourself more choices, grew, and came to understand why you were transformed. People are looking for universal experiences to help them make decisions.

Start by finding a newspaper reporter from a publication that is well-respected by the public, and have that person write about your life story experience or what you do with other peoples' life stories as a personal historian. That's the first step to introducing a 'salable' life story. The technique differs from writing a life story like a first-person diary novel for only your family and/or friends. With a 'salable' life story, you write about the universal experiences that connect all of us. If readers or viewers can identify with what you have to say, your words open doors for them to make decisions and choices by digesting your information.

The Proliferation of Writing Courses Online Targets Writing Your Life Story

The sheer number of classes on the Internet is like an explosion of education. You can now earn a masters degree in the techniques of teaching online from universities such as the California State University at Hayward in their continuing education department. What I see happening is that according to display ads in a variety of magazines of interest to writers, a proliferation of writing courses online has broken out.

How do you develop buzz appeal, pre-sell your book, create press coverage of their writing, all before you send it to a publisher or agent? A few years ago diaries were "in" just like several years before that the books about angels were "in style." What will be next?

Back in the year 2000, what enthralled readers included simple stories on how single parents put bread on the table, reared a family, and learned from their mistakes. What will be big in the future in publishing will be simple tales of what you learned, how you came to understand, and what you'll share with readers because what you learned from my mistakes helped you to grow and become a better person making the world a gentler place. Those books will be about values, virtues, and ethics in simple stories that help people heal. It will be universal stories with which we all can identify and use to solve problems and make decisions.

By the following year books showed readers how to have more choices and find more alternative solutions, more possibilities, and to find more information with which to solve problems and make decisions. A lot of those books will come from salable diaries and life stories as well as corporate histories and executive histories.

What was hot by 2002 was how people escaped domestic violence and made better choices through education and creativity enhancement. By 2003–2004 books focused on creativity enhancement and self-expression. The year 2003 became a utopia for books on creativity enhancement through personal experience and life story. You only have to look at the book lists in the publisher's magazines to see what the fad is for any one year and interview publishing professionals for the trends and directions for the following year.

Write about the human side of careers worked at for years. What did you retire to? How did you survive historic events, rear your family, or solve problems? The purpose of personal history writing can be, among other goals, to find closure. Those who can't use a hand-operated mouse and need to use a foot pedal mouse, breath straw, or other devices can still operate computers.

Others need assistance software to magnify the screen or audio software such as "Jaws," to hear as they type on keyboards. The idea is to use personal history and life story writing as a healing instrument to make contact with others, find this closure, relieve stress, to talk to parents long gone, to make decisions on how to grow, find understanding, learn from past mistakes, grow, and become a better person in one's own eyes.

Other students take a personal history, oral history, or life story writing classes to pass on to their grandchildren a script, a novel, a story, or a collage of their life experiences, and still others want corporate histories of how they founded their companies and became role models of success for business students to simulate, how they became successful giants for others to follow and benchmark.

Still other students are visionaries who want their life stories to be used to enhance the creativity of readers. Some of my students want to write their life story as a computer or board game on how they solved their own problems that are universal to all of us. And you have students who want careers as personal historians recording, transcribing, and preserving in a variety of formats the personal histories of individuals, families, corporations, art forms, and institutions.

Some are into conservation of videos, photographs, text material, tape recordings, CDs, DVDs, and other multimedia formats. All are involved in making time capsules for future researchers, historians, scholars, librarians, genealogists, and specialists who research personal and oral history or specialized history, such as music and art or rare books and manuscripts. Others are collectors. Most want a time capsule of a relative, complete with not only a relative's keepsake albums or video diary, but sometimes even a DNA printout for ancestry.

If you look in many publications of interest to writers, you might see online or correspondence courses offered to writers at American College of Journalism, Burlington College, Columbus University, specialists in distance education, or at Gotham Writers' Workshops at www.WritingClasses.com. There's Writers Digest School, and data bases where you can learn about agents at Agent Research & Evaluation, 334 E. 30, NYC, NY 10016 or on the Web at www.agentresearch.com. These are some of the online classes in writing advertised. You'll also see ads for classes in personal story writing in some of these publications.

You can get paid to teach what you love to do so much—share your writing techniques and write. Some writing schools online may put articles up on their trade journal online. And you can always sell articles to paying markets and use the clips with resumes. Thanks to the Internet—even a disabled teacher who isn't able to speak before a class for health reasons or drive to class, can teach and write online.

Personal history writing courses could also aim to show research on how creative writing can heal or have therapeutic qualities in gentle self-expression and quality circles online, and now I've found students who learn how to write a life story as therapy to heal and to find closure, solve problems, and to explore more choices, alternatives, and growth towards a kinder and gentler world.

You can focus strictly on recording, transcribing, and archiving people's or corporation's personal or oral histories and preserving them in a variety of formats as time capsules or target the more creative end of teaching writing personal histories as books, plays, or skits. In other words, you can be both a personal historian and a writing coach or focus on either career or business—oral and personal historian, or teacher of courses or "quality circles" in writing autobiographies and biographies for commercial markets.

You can start private classes on a mailing list and chat board. A fair price to charge could be about $80 per student for advanced workshops in writing salable material for 4-week courses with a 10-page critique per student. Your aim would be to be an online job coach in a writing or personal history career. Help students find ways to get into print by referring you them to resources. Show how to make writing more commercial. Reveal the techniques of effective story writing in your true story, biography, memoirs, autobiography, diary, journal, novel, story, play, or article.

A lot of biography writing is focused on interviews, whereas writing a diary or monologue focuses on inner reflections and expressions in explaining how you came to understand, learn from your past mistakes or experiences and good choices, and share how you solved problems, grew, and changed or were transformed.

Personal diaries start out with poetic-like descriptions of the senses, with lines such as "Cat shadow plump I arrive, carrying my Siamese kitten like a rifle through Spokane, while the only sensation I feel is my hair stretched like flaxen wires where my new kitten, Patches, hangs on. A gentle clock, the red beams of light reflected in his blue eyes remind me that my tattered self also must eat. His claws dig into my purse strap like golden flowers curling in unshaven armpits. I inhale his purrs like garlic, warm as the pap mom cat, Rada-Ring flowed into Patches nine weeks ago."

Have an enriching writing experience. I truly believe writing heals in some ways. It's a transformative experience like meditation or having the comforting feeling of watching a waterfall in natural settings or sitting in a garden of hanging green plants. Writing recharges my energy must like petting my kitten, Kokowellen, a Siamese while sitting my orchid garden listening to soothing melodies.

You might want to critique for pay, the pages of other people's writing of personal histories if they want to write for the commercial markets. In that case, critiquing may be done by email and online.

That way they don't send any hard copy to mail back or get lost. You always keep a copy. However, I recommend teaching online a course with the critique, as you'll get far more for your $80 for each ten pages of critiquing as a fair price, plus the tuition of the course as perhaps another $80.

The course provides resources, techniques, and ways to revise your material that helps you gain visibility. It's important to pre-sell your book and gain publicity for your writing before you send it off to a publisher or agent. You'll want to know how not to give too much away, but how to attract positive attention so people will eagerly look forward to hearing more from you.

Keep a separate mailing list for your online students. Make a mailing list.

Memoirs and diaries are in right now in the publishing world. It's not a passed fad, yet, like the angel books were a decade ago. If you're writing a diary, you want to write something in your first or second page after the opening that goes like this to be more commercial:

"Eagerness to learn grows on me. I see it reflected in the interviewers who stare at me, their enthusiasm is an approval of my expansive mind. I read so much now, just to look at the pages is to feel nourished. A kind of poetry turns into children's books on DVDs like a stalk that grows no where else is in season.

Creativity, like color, runs off my keyboard into the cooking water of my screen, drenched in pungent brainstorming. Writing online puts me in every farmer's kitchen. My computer has a good scent, and the stories written on its screen are apples bursting on the trees of my fingers. On my Web site, photos hang like lanterns. Teaching online ripens my stories. I analyze what effective storytelling means. Picture in three dimensions, pagodas of the mind."

If you come across writers block, try writing the lyrics to a song as a way to start writing your life story. You don't need to read notes, just fiddle with the words based upon an experience in time. Start by writing the ending first. Perhaps your title on salable diaries could be, "Pretty Little Secret," or "Ending the

Silence," or "Results of Promises," or "Guided by a Child's Silence," or "Unraveling a Tale," or "Bravery and Unspeakable Links," or "Unveiled, Unbridled, Unbound." My title was "Insight, Hindsight, Foresight."

9

Collecting Personal Histories

"Celebration of Life" Personal and Oral Histories Interviewing and Taping

People are "less camera shy" when two from the same peer group or class pair up and interview each other on video camcorder or on audio tape from a list of questions rehearsed. People also can write the questions they want to be asked and also write out and familiarize themselves with the answers alone and/or with their interviewers from their own peer group.

Some people have their favorite proverbs, or a logo that represents their outlook on life. Others have their own 'crusade' or mission. And some have a slogan that says what they are about in a few words...example, "seeking the joy of life," or "service with a smile."

Someone's motto, proverb, or slogan, for example, can form the foundation for a questionnaire on what they want to say in an oral history or personal history video or audio tape on in a multimedia presentation of their life story highlights. Here are some ways to interview people for personal history time capsules or how to inspire them to interview one another in a group setting or in front of a video camcorder in private with only interviewer and interviewee present.

And then there are those who want to tape themselves alone in their room or office with a camcorder on a tripod and a remote control device or a tape recorder and photographs. When records stop, there are always the DNA-driven genealogy and ancestry printouts.

Some people enjoy writing their life stories more than they like to speak about it. Or they prefer to read from a script as an audio tape. For those whose voices are impaired or for those who prefer to let a synthetic software voice tell their story, I recommend software such as TextAloud. This software allows anyone to cut and paste their writing from a disk such as a floppy disk, CD, DVD, or hard drive disk to the TextAloud software and select the type of voice to read their writing. With AT&T Natural Voices, you can select a male or female voice.

There are also voices with accents, such as a British accent male voice, and voice software available in a variety of languages to read writing in other languages. TextAloud is made by Nextup.com at the Web site: http://www. nextup.com/. According to their Web site, "TextAloud MP3 is Text-to-Speech software that uses voice synthesis to create spoken audio from text. You can listen on your PC or save text to MP3 or wave files for listening later." I play the MP3 files on my MP3 player.

I save the files to a CD as MP3 files. In this way I can turn my writing into audio books, pamphlets, or articles, poetry, plays, monologues, skits, or any form of writing read aloud by the synthetic software voice software. I save my audio files as MP3 files so I can play my personal history audio in my MP3 player on in my personal computer. MP3 files are condensed and take up a lot less room in your computer or on a Web site or CD and DVD disk than an audio .wav file.

If you're creating "celebration of life" oral or personal history audio tapes, it works well especially for those who prefer not to read their own writing aloud to a tape recorder. Although most people would like to hear their relatives' voices on tape in audio and video, some people are not able to read their works aloud to a recorder or camcorder. The synthetic voices will turn any type of writing saved on a disk as a text file into recorded voice—from short poetry to long-length books. The voices are usually recorded with Total Recorder software and saved as an MP3 file so they can be played on MP3 players or on most computers with CD players.

For those taping persons live in video to make time capsules or other keepsake albums in voice and/or video, it's best to let people think what they are going to say by handing them a list of a few questions. If you're working with a group of older adults, let one of the group members interview another group member by asking each question from a list of several questions.

Give someone a week's notice to come up with an answer to each question from a list of ten questions. Then give them two minutes to respond to each question by discussing how it relates to events in their lives or their experiences. You'll end up with a twenty minute video tape. If you allow only a minute for each question from a list of thirty questions, you have a thirty-minute tape.

Times may not be exact as people tend to elaborate to flesh out a question. Let the interview and interviewee practice before recording. So it's good to pair up two people. One will ask the interview questions, and the other will answer, talking about turning points and significant events in their lives.

They can be asked whether they have a personal proverb or slogan they live by or a motto or personal logo. Tapes can be anywhere from a half hour to an hour for life stories that can be saved as an MP3 file to a CD. Other files such as a Wave file (.wav) take up too much space on a CD. So they could be condensed into an MP3 file and saved that way. TextAloud and Total Recorder are software programs that save audio files. You can also use Music Match to convert .wav files to MP3 files.

I use TextAloud software and Total Recorder. Also I save the files as MP3 files for an audio CD that will also go up on a Web site. I use Windows Media Player to play the video files and save them as a Windows Media file (WMV file) so they can be easily uploaded to a Web site and still play in Windows Media Player that comes with Windows XP software.

When making time capsules in multimedia, I save on a CD and/or a DVD, and upload the file from my hard disk to a Web site. Copies of the CDs can be given to relatives, the interviewee, museums, libraries, and various schools who may be interested in oral history with a theme. Themes can be celebrations of life, living time capsules, or fit into any group theme under an umbrella title that holds them together.

This can be an era, such as living memories of a particular decade, life experiences in oral history of an area in geography, an ethnic group, or any other heading. Or the tapes can be of individuals or family groups. Not only life stories, but poetry, plays, novels, stories, and any other form of creative nonfiction or fiction writing can be recorded by synthetic voices as audio story or book collections. Some work well as children's stories and other types of writings as life stories or poetry.

Themes can vary from keepsake albums to time capsules to collections of turning points in history from the life stories of individuals. Also, themes can be recorded as "old time radio" programs or as oral military history from the experiences of veterans and notated to the Veterans History Project at the Library of Congress or other groups and museums. Make sure you have signed *release forms* that also release you from liability should any problems arise from putting someone's life story and name on the Web and/or donating it to a library or other public archive.

A good example of a release form is the one posted at the Veteran's History Project Web site where life stories of veterans are donated to the Library of Congress and accessible to the public for educational or scholarly research. Check out the .PDF release forms for both the interviewer and the interviewee at their Web site. The release form for veterans is at: <u>http://www.loc.gov/folklife/vets/vetform-vetrelease.pdf</u>.

10

Before Video Taping Life Stories of Older Adults: Questions to Ask Interviewing for Personal Histories: How to Interview Older Adults.

Intergenerational Writing for Genealogy and Life Stories.

STEP 1: Send someone enthusiastic about personal and oral history to senior community centers, lifelong learning programs at universities, nursing homes, or senior apartment complexes activity rooms. You can reach out to a wide variety of older adults in many settings, including at libraries, church groups, hobby and professional or trade associations, unions, retirement resorts, public transportation centers, malls, museums, art galleries, genealogy clubs, and intergenerational social centers.

STEP 2: Have each personal historian or volunteer bring a tape recorder with tape and a note pad. Bring camcorders for recording video to turn into time capsules and CDs or DVDs with life stories, personal history experiences, memoirs, and events highlighting turning points or special times in people's lives.

STEP 3: Assign each personal historian one or two older persons to interview with the following questions.

1. What were the most significant turning points or events in your life?

2.   How did you survive the Wars?

3.   What were the highlights, turning points, or significant events that you experienced during the economic downturn of 1929–1939? How did you cope or solve your problems?

4.   What did you do to solve your problems during the significant stages of your life at age 10, 20, 30, 40, 50, 60 and 70-plus? Or pick a year that you want to talk about.

5.   What changes in your life do you want to remember and pass on to future generations?

6.   What was the highlight of your life?

7.   How is it best to live your life after 70?

8.   What years do you remember most?

9.   What was your favorite stage of life?

10. What would you like people to remember about you and the times you lived through?

STEP 3:
Have the student record the older person's answers. Select the most significant events, experiences, or turning points the person chooses to emphasize. Then write the story of that significant event in ten pages or less.

STEP 4: Ask the older person to supply the younger student photos, art work, audio tapes, or video clips. Usually photos, pressed flowers, or art work will be supplied. Have the student or teacher scan the photos onto a disk and return the original photos or art work or music to the owner.

STEP 5:The personal historian, volunteer, student and/or teacher scans the photos and puts them onto a Web site on the Internet at one of the free communities that give away Web site to the public at no cost….some include http://www. tripod.com , http://www.fortunecity.com , http://www.angelfire.com , http:// www.geocities.com , and others. Most search engines will give a list of communities at offering free Web sites to the public. Microsoft also offers free family Web sites for family photos and newsletters or information. Ask your Internet service provider whether it offers free Web site space to subscribers. The free Web sites are limited in space.

For larger Web site spaces with room for audio and video material and other keepsake memorabilia, purchase a personal Web site from a Web-hosting company. Shop around for affordable Web site space for a multimedia life story time capsule that would include text, video and/or audio clips, music, art, photos, and any other effects.

1. Create a Web site with text from the older person's significant life events

2. Add photos.

3. Add sound or .wav files with the voice of the older person speaking in small clips or sound bites.

4. Intersperse text and photos or art work with sound, if available.

   Add video clips, if available and won't take too much bandwidth.

5. Put Web site on line as TIME CAPSULE of (insert name of person) interviewed and edited by, insert name of student who interviewed older person.

STEP 6: Label each Web site Time Capsule and collect them in a history archives on the lives of older adults at the turn of the millennium. Make sure the older person and all relatives and friends are emailed the Web site link. You have now created a time capsule for future generations.

This can be used as a classroom exercise in elementary and high schools to teach the following:

1. Making friends with older adults.

2. Learning to write on intergenerational topics.

3. Bringing community together of all generations.

4. Learning about foster grandparents.

5. History lessons from those who lived through history.

6. Learning about diversity and how people of diverse origins lived through the 20th century.

7. Preserving the significant events in the lives of people as time capsules for future generations to know what it was like to live between 1900 and 2000 at any age.

8. Learning to write skits and plays from the life stories of older adults taken down by young students.

9. Teaching older adults skills in creative writing at senior centers.

10. Learning what grandma did during World War 2 or the stock market crash of 1929 followed by the economic downturn of 1930–1938.

What to Ask People about Their Lives

Step 1

When you interview, ask for facts and concrete details. Look for statistics, and research whether statistics are deceptive in your case.

Step 2

To write a plan, write one sentence for each topic that moves the story or piece forward. Then summarize for each topic in a paragraph. Use dialogue at least in every third paragraph.

Step 3

Look for the following facts or headings to organize your plan for a biography or life story.

1. PROVERB. Ask the people you interview what would be their proverb or slogan if they had to create/invent a slogan that fit themselves or their aspirations: One slogan might be something like the seventies ad for cigarettes, "We've come a long way, baby," to signify ambition. Only look for an original slogan.

2. PURPOSE. Ask the people you interview or a biography, for what purpose is or was their journey? Is or was it equality in the workplace or something personal and different such as dealing with change—downsizing, working after retirement, or anything else?

3. IMPRINT. Ask what makes an imprint or impact on people's lives and what impact the people you're interviewing want to make on others?

4. STATISTICS: How deceptive are they? How can you use them to focus on reality?

5. How have the people that you're interviewing influenced changes in the way people or corporations function?

6. To what is the person aspiring?

7. What kind of communication skills does the person have and how are these skills received? Are the communication skills male or female, thinking or feeling, yin or yang, soft or steeled, and are people around these people negative or positive about those communication skills?

8. What new styles is the person using? What kind of motivational methods, structure, or leadership? Is the person a follower or leader? How does the person match his or her personality to the character of a corporation or interest?

9. How does the person handle change?

10. How is the person reinforced?

Once you have titles and summarized paragraphs for each segment of your story, you can more easily flesh out the story by adding dialogue and description to your factual information. Look for differences in style between the people you interview? How does the person want to be remembered?

Is the person a risk taker or cautious for survival? Does the person identify with her job or the people involved in the process of doing the work most creatively or originally? Does creative expression take precedence over processes of getting work out to the right place at the right time? Does the person want his ashes to spell the words "re-invent yourself" where the sea meets the shore? This is a popular concept appearing in various media.

Search the Records in the Family History Library of Salt Lake City, Utah

Make use of the database online at the Family History Library of Salt Lake City, Utah. Or visit the branches in many locations. The Family History Library (FHL) is known worldwide as the focal point of family history records preservation.

The FHL collection contains more than 2.2 million rolls of microfilmed genealogical records, 742,000 microfiche, 300,000 books, and 4,500 periodicals that represent data collected from over 105 countries. You don't have to be a member of any particular church or faith to use the library or to go online and search the records.

Family history records owe a lot to the invention of writing. And then there is oral history, but someone needs to transcribe oral history to record and archive them for the future.

Interestingly, isn't it a coincidence that writing is 6,000 years old and DNA that existed 6,000 years ago first reached such crowded conditions in the very cities that had first used writing extensively to measure accounting and trade had very little recourse but to move on to new areas where there were far less people and less use of writing?

A lot of major turning points occurred 6,000 years ago—the switch to a grain-based diet from a meat and root diet, the use of bread and fermented grain beverages, making of oil from plants, and the rise of religions based on building "god houses" in the centers of town in areas known as the "cereal belt" around the world.

Six thousand years ago in India we have the start of the Sanskrit writings, the cultivation of grain. In China, we have the recording of acupuncture points for medicine built on energy meridians that also show up in the blue tattoos of the Ice Man fossil "Otsi" in the Alps—along the same meridians as the Chinese acupuncture points.

At 6,000 years ago the Indo European languages spread out across Europe. Mass migrations expanded by the Danube leaving pottery along the trade routes that correspond to the clines and gradients of gene frequency coming out of the cereal belts.

Then something happened. There was an agricultural frontier cutting off the agriculturists from the hunters. Isn't it a coincidence that the agricultural frontiers or barriers also are genetic barriers at least to some degree?

Oral History

Here's how to systematically collect, record, and preserve living peoples' testimonies about their own experiences. After you record in audio and/or video the highlights of anyone's experiences, try to verify your findings. See whether you can check any facts in order to find out whether the person being recorded is making up the story or whether it really did happen.

This is going to be difficult unless you have witnesses or other historical records. Once you have verified your findings to the best of your ability, note whether the findings have been verified. Then analyze what you found. Put the oral history recordings in an accurate historical context.

Mark the recordings with the dates and places. Watch where you store your findings so scholars in the future will be able to access the transcript or recording and convert the recording to another, newer technology. For instance, if you have a transcript on paper, have it saved digitally on a disk and somewhere else on tape and perhaps a written transcript on acid-free good paper in case technology moves ahead before the transcript or recording is converted to the new technology.

For example, if you only put your recording on a phonograph record, within a generation or two, there may not be any phonographs around to play the record. The same goes for CDs, DVDs and audio or video tapes.

So make sure you have a readable paper copy to be transcribed or scanned into the new technology as well as the recordings on disk and tape. For example, if you record someone's experiences in a live interview with your video camera, use a cable to save the video in the hard disk of a computer and then burn the file to a CD or DVD.

Keep a copy of audio tape and a copy of regular video tape—all in a safe place such as a time capsule, and make a copy for various archives in libraries and university oral history preservation centers. Be sure scholars in the future can find a way to enjoy the experiences in your time capsule, scrapbook, or other storage device for oral histories.

Use your DNA testing results to add more information to a historical record. As an interviewer with a video camera and/or audio tape recorder, your task is to record as a historical record what the person who you are interviewing recollects.

The events move from the person being interviewed to you, the interviewer, and then into various historical records. In this way you can combine results of DNA testing with actual memories of events. If it's possible, also take notes or have someone take notes in case the tape doesn't pick up sounds clearly.

I had the experience of having a video camera battery go out in spite of all precautions when I was interviewing someone, and only the audio worked. So keep a backup battery on hand whether you use a tape recorder or a video camera. If at all possible, have a partner bring a spare camera and newly recharged battery. A fully charged battery left overnight has a good chance of going out when you need it.

11

Family and Faith: What's in an Oral History?

Emphasize the commitment to family and faith. To create readers' and media attention to an oral history, it should have some redemptive value to a universal audience. That's the most important point. Make your oral history simple and earthy. Write about real people who have values, morals, and a faith in something greater than themselves that is equally valuable to readers or viewers.

Publishers who buy an oral history written as a book on its buzz value are buying simplicity. It is simplicity that sells and nothing else but simplicity. This is true for oral histories, instructional materials, and fiction. It's good storytelling to say it simply.

Simplicity means the oral history or memoirs book or story gives you all the answers you were looking for in your life in exotic places, but found it close by. What's the great proverb that your oral history is telling the world?

Is it to stand on your own two feet and put bread on your own table for your family? That's the moral point, to pull your own weight, and pulling your own weight is a buzz word that sells oral histories and fiction that won't preach, but instead teach and reach through simplicity.

That's the backbone of the oral historian's new media. Buzz means the story is simple to understand. You make the complex easier to grasp. And buzz means you can sell your story or book, script or narrative by focusing on the values of simplicity, morals, faith, and universal values that hold true for everyone.

Doing the best to take care of your family sells and is buzz appeal, hot stuff in the publishing market of today and in the oral history archives. This is true, regardless of genre. Publishers go through fads every two years—angel books, managing techniques books, computer home-based business books, novels about ancient historical characters or tribes, science fiction, children's programming, biography, and oral history transcribed into a book or play.

The genres shift emphasis, but values are consistent in the bestselling books. Perhaps your oral history will be simple enough to become a bestselling book or script. In the new media, simplicity is buzz along with values. Oral history, like best-selling novels and true stories is built on simplicity, values, morals, and commitment. Include how one person dealt with about trends. Focus your own oral history about life in the lane of your choice. Develop one central issue and divide that issue into a few important questions that highlight or focus on that one central issue.

When you write or speak a personal history either alone or in an interview, you focus on determining the order of your life story. Don't use flashbacks. Focus on the highlights and turning points. Organize what you'll say or write. An autobiography deals in people's relationships. Your autobiography deals as much with what doesn't change—the essentials—as what life changes you and those around you go through.

Your autobiography should be more concrete than abstract. You want the majority of people to understand what you mean. Say what you mean, and mean what you say. More people understand concrete details than understand abstract ideas.

Be personal in a life story. The more personal you are, the more eternal is your life story. More people will view or read it again and again far into the future. You can emphasize your life's journey and look at the world through your own eyes. To make the structure salable, 'meander' your life as you would travel on a journey. Perhaps you're a winding river meandering around obstacles and competitors. At each stop, you learn your own capabilities and your own place in the world.

The more you meander, the more you take away the urgency from your story that sets up tension in the audience and keeps them on the edge of their seat. Don't let the meandering overpower your sense of urgency. Don't dwell on your reaction. Focus on your action to people and situations. Stay active in your own personal history. In other words, don't repeat how you reacted, but show how you acted.

Before you sit down to write your autobiography, think of yourself in terms of going on a journey inside the privacy of your purse or wallet. May your purse is the only place where you really do have any privacy. Come up for air when you have hit bottom. Bob up to the sunshine, completely changed or at least matured. If you have really grown, you will not be blinded by the light, in the figurative sense, as the song goes. Instead, the light gives you insight. So now you have vision along with some hindsight. The next step is learning how to promote and market your salable personal history or life story.

A biography reports the selected events of another person's life—usually 12 major events in the six various significant events also known as "turning points" and also known as "transition points" of life that would include the highlights of significant events for each of the six stages of growth: 1) infanthood, 2) childhood, 3) teen years 4) young adulthood 5)middle life 6)maturity.

Is Your Life Story A Dialogue With Your Higher Self?

If your autobiography has punch and power, is marketable and makes viewers want to network and discuss it in quality circles, you life story will make a concrete impact on the abstract idea of diary writing. Some pause to write from introspection and reflection. Others prefer to write action from biography. Your mission, should you decide to broadcast it, is to locate business people who want to buy or sell a true life story. It's as profitable for them as it's a healing experience for you if you see it as an exercise in getting to know yourself. Writing and recording your personal history is a search for your core identity.

Personal history writing and speaking or recording reminds me of Stan Dale's quote, "Intimacy is spelled "in to me you see." The quote also is listed on the *New Intimacy* Web site at http://www.menstuff.org/columns/newintimacy/52.html.

Writing personal history is writing about intimacy. An autobiography helps you practice seeing another person with your soul. Writing the life story offers you a vitality. In the writing process, you see who you are and make a connection with others who shaped your world as you, in turn, shaped the world of those around you.

When you write your autobiography, listen with your body. One of the conclusions many autobiography writers arrive at is "I am never enough." This decision isn't commercial, although the story line with an upbeat ending is marketable. The "not enough" feeling you write in your diary creates fear and loneliness. What would happen if you took a plot line of a protagonist who says: "I'm not enough or give me a break" and linked it with an antagonist who says: "I need a connection." You have opposites, perhaps a couple. One says, "I need a break." The other replies, "Not until I have a connection."

Then you use one-liners in the dialogue. "Give me a break" could mask profound loneliness with a tough outer shell (as in I don't need anybody). Your antagonist might continue with a response that repeated "Not without a connection."

The dialogue would be between two people who want a relationship so eagerly that one of them could be more willing to openly work lovingly for it. Your premise would be that the protagonist is really saying, "I don't know how to connect." The audience sees the deep suffering and the false armor in dialogue and visual action. Not everyone wants other people in a personal history. Do you really want you and your competition in your personal history video? Not unless you're making a feature film about your life.

In reality, you can sell your life story to a small press publisher, to an independent, low-budget producer, or produce it as a play for a few thousand dollars in a local theatre. The least expensive way to handle a personal history is to put it on a DVD and on a CD. Have a text copy, and if you have a Web site, upload the video clip and text to the Web as a time capsule. Designate someone to take over the payments on the Web site when you can no longer maintain it. You can even rent an option to someone else's life story's movie rights.

If you want power over your life story, look at the structure of your personal history. If you know you have a salable story, how many ways can you market your autobiographical or biographical writing? One way to market your story is by utilizing interactive computer software to help yourself and others to write their own life events document. There are several computer software disks on the market that will organize your life story events. You can form quality circles and teach life story writing to groups, including adult education classes and at senior community centers.

Will Computer Software Help You Write Your Life Story?

You may first wish to market your autobiography on computer software disks. Interactive fiction is a writing game recorded on a computer floppy disk which allows the player to answer questions, but the easiest way is to put your video on a DVD.

There are alternative answers. This game is suitable for playing "What if I chose the road not taken? What would my life story be like, then?" To create and market an interactive fiction autobiography game, hire an independent programmer who specializes in programming floppy disk software with questions and alternative answers.

Turn a keepsake album into a time capsule. Put your life story on the Web or on a DVD and CD. Then publish it as a book or as a print-on-demand book or booklet. Self-publishing will give you the electronic and audio rights to your book. With print-on-demand publishing, you may lose your electronic rights depending on which publisher you use. Or buy print-on-demand software and publish your own books as a print-on-demand publication. Check out your contract.

You can work with printers and use print-on-demand software or send your book by email to a print-on-demand publisher who for a fee, in many cases, does all the work and distribution, but not the promotion. You do your own promotion and publicity.

If you go the way of complicated interactive story writing, you'll need to work with someone who knows how to create interactive stories. When a player is interactive, it means he/she interacts with the computer in a learning situation.

For example, the computer software could be designed to ask you these following questions: "What if you chose to become a paralegal instead of a full-time freelance writer? Would freelance writers have the starving artist mentality? What if your fiction always has been rejected? What if you are totally dependent on relatives for support? Where would you be working today?

Would you be happy? How much would you be earning? Who would you meet and marry? Would he/she be kind or abusive? Would you be a co-dependent seeking to be parented?

Interactive software allows you to play the possibilities or create new realities in the present. You can team up with a programmer. Another alternative is using strictly autobiographical software to organize your life story like a diary. You can look back on the result and judge whether it is commercial or strictly for the family genealogy collection.

You may wish to use software to organize your own life story and print out a document. Some story organizing software breaks your history into manageable sections. In fact, some story writing software offer more than 400 specific questions to prompt you to provide details of each area of your life. If you use this type of software, you answer by keyboarding in all the important details into your computer. Then you save it on a disk for posterity. Answer only the questions you choose.

The programs work by advancing one screen at a time when you feel like it. You can spend years writing your autobiography or just a few days. The programs include topics such as your birth, medical events, friends, education, property, holidays, achievements, and other categories. These types of story writing programs might organize various categories and the facts in them so you can glance at your life and decide whether to turn it into a novel, a screenplay, a stage play, video, radio play, audio, or leave it as a book for the family eyes only.

When you're finished typing in the details of each event, you can print your story or export the file to your word processing program or desktop publishing software for formatting into a small tale or a full document. Some of these programs allow you to write a large number of pages, even up to 3,000 pages.

You can print out the document and have it bound in a cover by a photocopying company. Then present it to each family member as a holiday gift. You can use this document to set the record straight, to write your memoirs, or to create every detail of your life or any one else's life for relatives or for history.

Long after you're gone, your descendants will read it. You can even explain why you included or excluded certain relatives out of your will.

You can pass on information about your marriage to your children so they would repeat or avoid the same choices based on the events of your early childhood programming or whatever you choose to detail. Public domain software offers various programs on creating diaries and life events on software. For other types of software consult software catalogues, public domain software listings, computer bulletin boards and trade journals.

Software can be used two ways: 1: To sell your own autobiography interactive games or 2: To organize and print out your own life events by answering interactive questions on already existing autobiography-writing software. Desktop video combines computer software, burning files to DVD and/or CDs, and transferring videotape played on your VCR to DVD disks. Sometimes desktop publishing combines with desktop video also known as multimedia authoring.

You may choose to create video programs that can be used interactively with computer software to ask someone hundreds of questions about autobiographical events. I like putting material on CDs or DVDs and mailing them to my online students when I used to teach university-level writing and speaking courses entirely online.

If you're a facilitator, you can help others to write, illustrate or to express themselves in multimedia. Writing personal histories interactively with video interviews, DVDs, the Web, and multimedia instruction on computers for beginners works very well with senior citizens. Use videobiography techniques in an autobiography writing class. Use assisted living recreational centers and community centers or adult education classrooms and meeting rooms in public parks and libraries.

Psychotherapists will also find this introspective way of writing works well with clients who would rather share their innermost thoughts and details of life events with a computer. To protect the privacy of people, it's a good way of "getting thoughts and feelings off your chest in words.

When you go public, ask yourself how your researched information can be of help to others who seek your information for making choices and decisions in their own lives. Personal history writing also helps you seek self-identity and share your introspective feelings on paper or through interviews on video or audio without direct contact with a group. You can dialogue with the questions on the computer in total privacy.

12

Steps to Take in Gathering Oral Histories

Use the following sequence when gathering oral/aural histories:

1. Develop one central issue and divide that issue into a few important questions that highlight or focus on that one central issue.

2. Write out a plan just like a business plan for your oral history project. You may have to use that plan later to ask for a grant for funding, if required. Make a list of all your products that will result from the oral history when it's done.

3. Write out a plan for publicity or public relations and media relations. How are you going to get the message to the public or special audiences?

4. Develop a budget. This is important if you want a grant or to see how much you'll have to spend on creating an oral history project.

5. List the cost of video taping and editing, packaging, publicity, and help with audio or special effects and stock shot photos of required.

6. What kind of equipment will you need? List that and the time slots you give to each part of the project. How much time is available? What are your deadlines?

7. What's your plan for a research? How are you going to approach the people to get the interviews? What questions will you ask?

8. Do the interviews. Arrive prepared with a list of questions. It's okay to ask the people the kind of questions they would like to be asked. Know what dates the interviews will cover in terms of time. Are you covering the economic depression of the thirties? World Wars? Fifties? Sixties? Pick the time parameters.

9. Edit the interviews so you get the highlights of experiences and events, the important parts. Make sure what's important to you also is important to the person you interviewed.

10. Find out what the interviewee wants to emphasize perhaps to highlight events in a life story. Create a video-biography of the highlights of one person's life or an oral history of an event or series of events.

11. Process audio as well as video, and make sure you have written transcripts of anything on audio and/or video in case the technology changes or the tapes go bad.

12. Save the tapes to compact disks, DVDs, a computer hard disk and several other ways to preserve your oral history time capsule. Donate any tapes or CDs to appropriate archives, museums, relatives of the interviewee, and one or more oral history libraries. They are usually found at universities that have an oral history department and library such as UC Berkeley and others.

13. Check the Web for oral history libraries at universities in various states and abroad.

14. Evaluate what you have edited. Make sure the central issue and central questions have been covered in the interview. Find out whether newspapers or magazines want summarized transcripts of the audio and/or video with photos.

15. Contact libraries, archives, university oral history departments and relevant associations and various ethnic genealogy societies that focus on the subject matter of your central topic.

16. Keep organizing what you have until you have long and short versions of your oral history for various archives and publications. Contact magazines and newspapers to see whether editors would assign reporters to do a story on the oral history project.

17. Create a scrapbook with photos and summarized oral histories. Write a synopsis of each oral history on a central topic or issue. Have speakers give public presentations of what you have for each person interviewed and/or for the entire project using highlights of several interviews with the media for publicity. Be sure your project is archived properly and stored in a place devoted to oral history archives and available to researchers and authors.

Aural/Oral History Techniques

1. Begin with easy to answer questions that don't require you explore and probe deeply in your first question. Focus on one central issue when asking questions. Don't use abstract questions. A plain question would be "What's your purpose?" An abstract question with connotations would be "What's your crusade?" Use questions with denotations instead of connotations. Keep questions short and plain—easy to understand. Examples would be, "What did you want to accomplish? How did you solve those problems? How did you find closure?" Ask the familiar "what, when, who, where, how, and why."

2. First research written or visual resources before you begin to seek an oral history of a central issue, experience, or event.

3. Who is your intended audience?

4. What kind of population niche or sample will you target?

5. What means will you select to choose who you will interview? What group of people will be central to your interview?

6. Write down how you'll explain your project. Have a script ready so you don't digress or forget what to say on your feet.

7. Consult oral history professionals if you need more information. Make sure what you write in your script will be clear to understand by your intended audience.

8. Have all the equipment you need ready and keep a list of what you'll use and the cost. Work up your budget.

9. Choose what kind of recording device is best—video, audio, multimedia, photos, and text transcript. Make sure your video is broadcast quality. I use a Sony Digital eight (high eight) camera.

10. Make sure from cable TV stations or news stations that what type of video and audio you choose ahead of time is broadcast quality.

11. Make sure you have an external microphone and also a second microphone as a second person also tapes the interview in case the quality of your camera breaks down. You can also keep a tape recorder going to capture the audio in case your battery dies.

12. Make sure your battery is fully charged right before the interview. Many batteries die down after a day or two of nonuse.

13. Test all equipment before the interview and before you leave your office or home. I've had batteries go down unexpectedly and happy there was another person ready with another video camera waiting and also an audio tape version going.

14. Make sure the equipment works if it's raining, hot, cold, or other weather variations. Test it before the interview. Practice interviewing someone on your equipment several times to get the hang of it before you show up at the interview.

15. Make up your mind how long the interview will go before a break and use tape of that length, so you have one tape for each segment of the interview. Make several copies of your interview questions.

16. Be sure the interviewee has a copy of the questions long before the interview so the person can practice answering the questions and think of what to say or even take notes. Keep checking your list of what you need to do.

17. Let the interviewee make up his own questions if he wants. Perhaps your questions miss the point. Present your questions first. Then let him embellish the questions or change them as he wants to fit the central issue with his own experiences.

18. Call the person two days and then one day before the interview to make sure the individual will be there on time and understands how to travel to the

location. Or if you are going to the person's home, make sure you understand how to get there.

19. Allow yourself one extra hour in case of traffic jams.

20. Choose a quiet place. Turn off cell phones and any ringing noises. Make sure you are away from barking dogs, street noise, and other distractions.

21. Before you interview make sure the person knows he or she is going to be video and audio-taped.

22. If you don't want anyone swearing, make that clear it's for public archives and perhaps broadcast to families.

23. Your interview questions should follow the journalist's information-seeking format of asking, who, what, where, where, how, and why. Oral history is a branch of journalistic research.

24. Let the person talk and don't interrupt. You be the listener and think of oral history as aural history from your perspective.

25. Make sure only one person speaks without being interrupted before someone else takes his turn to speak.

26. Understand silent pauses are for thinking of what to say.

27. Ask one question and let the person gather his thoughts.

28. Finish all your research on one question before jumping to the next question. Keep it organized by not jumping back to the first question after the second is done. Stay in a linear format.

29. Follow up what you can about any one question, finish with it, and move on to the next question without circling back. Focus on listening instead of asking rapid fire questions as they would confuse the speaker.

30. Ask questions that allow the speaker to begin to give a story, anecdote, life experience, or opinion along with facts. Don't ask questions that can be answered only be yes or no. This is not a courtroom. Let the speaker elaborate with facts and feelings or thoughts.

31. Late in the interview, start to ask questions that explore and probe for deeper answers.

32. Wrap up with how the person solved the problem, achieved results, reached a conclusion, or developed an attitude, or found the answer. Keep the wrap-up on a light, uplifting note.

33. Don't leave the individual hanging in emotion after any intensity of. Respect the feelings and opinions of the person. He or she may see the situation from a different point of view than someone else. So respect the person's right to feel as he does. Respect his need to recollect his own experiences.

34. Interview for only one hour at a time. If you have only one chance, interview for an hour. Take a few minutes break. Then interview for the second hour. Don't interview more than two hours at any one meeting.

35. Use prompts such as paintings, photos, music, video, diaries, vintage clothing, crafts, antiques, or memorabilia when appropriate. Carry the photos in labeled files or envelopes to show at appropriate times in order to prime the memory of the interviewee.

    For example, you may show a childhood photo and ask "What was it like in that orphanage where these pictures were taken?" Or travel photos might suggest a trip to America as a child, or whatever the photo suggests.

    Ask questions such as: "Do you remember when this ice cream parlor inside the ABC movie house stood at the corner of X and Y Street? Did you go there as a teenager? What was your funniest memory of this movie theater or the ice cream store inside back in the fifties?"

36. As soon as the interview is over, label all the tapes and put the numbers in order.

37. A signed release form is required before you can broadcast anything. So have the interviewee sign a release form before the interview.

38. Make sure the interviewee gets a copy of the tape and a transcript of what he or she said on tape. If the person insists on making corrections, send the paper transcript of the tape for correction to the interviewee. Edit the tape as best you can or have it edited professionally.

39. Make sure you comply with all the corrections the interviewee wants changed. He or she may have given inaccurate facts that need to be corrected on the paper transcript.

40. Have the tape edited with the corrections, even if you have to make a tape at the end of the interviewee putting in the corrections that couldn't be edited out or changed.

41. As a last resort, have the interviewee redo the part of the tape that needs correction and have it edited in the tape at the correct place marked on the tape. Keep the paper transcript accurate and up to date, signed with a release form by the interviewee.

42. Oral historians write a journal of field notes about each interview. Make sure these get saved and archived so they can be read with the transcript.

43. Have the field notes go into a computer where someone can read them along with the transcript of the oral history tape or CD.

44. Thank the interviewee in writing for taking the time to do an interview for broadcast and transcript.

45. Put a label on everything you do from the interview to the field notes. Make a file and sub file folders and have everything stored in a computer, in archived storage, and in paper transcript.

46. Make copies and digital copies of all photos and put into the records in a computer. Return originals to owners.

47. Make sure you keep your fingerprints off the photos by wearing white cotton gloves. Use cardboard when sending the photos back and pack securely. Also photocopy the photos and scan the photos into your computer. Treat photos as antique art history in preservation.

48. Make copies for yourself of all photos, tapes, and transcripts. Use your duplicates, and store the original as the master tape in a place that won't be used often, such as a time capsule or safe, or return to a library or museum where the original belongs.

49. Return all original photos to the owners. An oral history archive library or museum also is suitable for original tapes. Use copies only to work from, copy, or distribute.

50. Index your tapes and transcripts. To use oral history library and museum terminology, recordings and transcripts are given "accession numbers."

51. Phone a librarian in an oral history library of a university for directions on how to assign accession numbers to your tapes and transcripts if the materials are going to be stored at that particular library. Store copies in separate places in case of loss or damage.

52. If you don't know where the materials will be stored, use generic accession numbers to label your tapes and transcripts. Always keep copies available for yourself in case you have to duplicate the tapes to send to an institution, museum, or library, or to a broadcast company.

53. Make synopses available to public broadcasting radio and TV stations.

54. Check your facts.

55. Are you missing anything you want to include?

56. Is there some place you want to send these tapes and transcripts such as an ethnic museum, radio show, or TV satellite station specializing in the topics on the tapes, such as public TV stations? Would it be suitable for a world music station? A documentary station?

57. If you need more interviews, arrange them if possible.

58. Give the interviewee a copy of the finished product with the corrections. Make sure the interviewee signs a release form that he or she is satisfied with the corrections and is releasing the tape to you and your project.

59. Store the tapes and transcripts in a library or museum or at a university or other public place where it will be maintained and preserved for many generations and restored when necessary.

60. You can also send copies to a film repository or film library that takes video tapes, an archive for radio or audio tapes for radio broadcast or cable TV.

61. Copies may be sent to various archives for storage that lasts for many generations. Always ask whether there are facilities for restoring the tape. A museum would most likely have these provisions as would a large library that has an oral history library project or section.

62. Make sure the master copy is well protected and set up for long-term storage in a place where it will be protected and preserved.

63. If the oral history is about events in history, various network news TV stations might be interested. Film stock companies may be interested in copies of old photos.

64. Find out from the subject matter what type of archives, repository, or storage museums and libraries would be interested in receiving copies of the oral history tapes and transcripts.

65. Print media libraries would be interested in the hard paper copy transcripts and photos as would various ethnic associations and historical preservation societies. Find out whether the materials will go to microfiche, film, or be digitized and put on CDs and DVDs, or on the World Wide Web.

If you want to create a time capsule for the Web, you can ask the interviewee whether he or she wants the materials or selected materials to be put online or on CD as multimedia or other. Then you would get a signed release from the interviewee authorizing you to put the materials or excerpts online.

Also find out in whose name the materials are copyrighted and whether you have print and electronic rights to the material or do the owners-authors-interviewees—or you, the videographer-producer? Get it all in writing, signed by those who have given you any interviews, even if you have to call your local intellectual property rights attorney.

How Accurate Are Oral Histories?

Cameras give fragments, points of view, and bits and pieces. Viewers will see what the videographer or photographer intends to be seen. The interviewee will also be trying to put his point of view across and tell the story from his perspective. Will the photographer or videographer be in agreement with the interviewee? Or if you are recording for print transcript, will your point of view agree with the interviewee's perspective and experience if your basic 'premise,' where you two are coming from, are not in agreement? Think this over as you write your list of questions. Do both of you agree on your central issue on which you'll focus for the interview?

How are you going to turn spoken words into text for your paper hard copy transcript? Will you transcribe verbatim, correct the grammar, or quote as you hear the spoken words? Oral historians really need to transcribe the exact spoken word. You can leave out the 'ahs' and 'oms' or loud pauses, as the interviewee thinks what to say next. You don't want to sound like a court reporter, but you do want to have an accurate record transcribed of what was spoken.

You're also not editing for a movie, unless you have permission to turn the oral history into a TV broadcast, where a lot gets cut out of the interview for time constraints. For that, you'd need written permission so words won't be taken out of context and strung together in the editing room to say something different from what the interviewee intended to say.

Someone talking could put in wrong names, forget what they wanted to say, or repeat themselves. They could mumble, ramble, or do almost anything. So you would have to sit down and weed out redundancy when you can or decide on presenting exactly what you've heard as transcript.

When someone reads the transcript in text, they won't have what you had in front of you, and they didn't see and hear the live presentation or the videotape. It's possible to misinterpret gestures or how something is spoken, the mood or tone, when reading a text transcript. Examine all your sources. Use an ice-breaker to get someone talking.

If a woman is talking about female-interest issues, she may feel more comfortable talking to another woman. Find out whether the interviewee is more comfortable speaking to someone of his or her own age. Some older persons feel they can relate better to someone close to their own age than someone in high school, but it varies. Sometimes older people can speak more freely to a teenager.

The interviewee must be able to feel comfortable with the interviewer and know he or she will not be judged. Sometimes it helps if the interviewer is the same ethnic group or there is someone present of the same group or if new to the language, a translator is present.

Read some books on oral history field techniques. Read the National Genealogical Society Quarterly (NGSQ). Also look at The American Genealogist (TAG), The Genealogist, and The New England Historical and Genealogical Register (The Register). If you don't know the maiden name of say, your grandmother's mother, and no relative knows either because it wasn't on her death certificate, try to reconstruct the lives of the males who had ever met the woman whose maiden name is unknown.

Maybe she did business with someone before marriage or went to school or court. Someone may have recorded the person's maiden name before her marriage. Try medical records if any were kept. There was no way to find my mother's grandmother's maiden name until I started searching to see whether she had any brothers in this country. She had to have come as a passenger on a ship around 1880 as she bought a farm. Did her husband come with her?

Was the farm in his name? How many brothers did she have in this country with her maiden surname? If the brothers were not in this country, what countries did they come from and what cities did they live in before they bought the farm in Albany? If I could find out what my great grandmother's maiden name was through any brothers living at the time, I could contact their descendants perhaps and see whether any male or female lines are still in this country or where else on the globe.

Perhaps a list of midwives in the village at the time is recorded in a church or training school for midwives. Fix the person in time and place. Find out whom she might have done business with and whether any records of that business exist. What businesses did she patronize? Look for divorce or court records, change of name records, and other legal documents.

Look at local sources. Did anyone save records from bills of sale for weddings, purchases of homes, furniture, debutante parties, infant supplies, or even medical records? Look at nurses' licenses, midwives' registers, employment contracts, and teachers' contracts, alumni associations for various schools, passports, passenger lists, alien registration cards, naturalization records, immigrant aid societies, city directories, and cross-references. Try religious and women's clubs, lineage and village societies, girl scouts and similar groups, orphanages, sanatoriums, hospitals, police records. Years ago there was even a Eugenics Record Office. What about the women's prisons? The first one opened in 1839—Mount Pleasant Female Prison, NY.

Try voters' lists. If your relative is from another country, try records in those villages or cities abroad. Who kept the person's diaries? Have you checked the Orphan Train records? Try ethnic and religious societies and genealogy associations for that country. Most ethnic genealogy societies have a special interest group for even the smallest villages in various countries.

You can start one and put up a Web site for people who also come from there in past centuries. Check alimony, divorce, and court records, widow's pensions of veterans, adoptions, orphanages, foster homes, medical records, birth, marriage, and death certificates, social security, immigration, pet license owners' files, prisons, alumni groups from schools, passenger lists, military, and other legal records.

When all historical records are being tied together, you can add the DNA testing to link all those cousins. Check military pensions on microfilms in the National Archives. See the bibliography section of this book for further resources on highly recommended books and articles on oral history field techniques and similar historical subjects.

13

Document Rescue and Recovery

Rescue and Recover Diaries, Bibles, and Old Family Cookbooks

Here's how to "mend conditions" and restore diaries. First make a book jacket for a diary. Put a title and label on the dust jacket with the name of the diary's author and any dates, city, state, or country.

Use acid-free paper for the jacket. Diaries and book jackets are works of art. If torn, mend the diary. Apply a protective plastic wrapper to your valuable dust jacket or give diaries dust jackets in good condition.

Be cautious using bleach, because chlorine fumes will fade the ink and soak through the opposite page to fade that writing. After testing the bleach, if the diary is dingy and dirty, bleach it white on the edges only using diluted bleach that won't fade old ink. Test the bleach first on similar surfaces, such as a blank page in the book.

Repair old diaries, and turn them into heirlooms for families and valuable collectibles. The current price for repairing handwritten diaries and books is about $50 and up per book or bound diary. Better yet, publish diaries as print-on-demand PDF files and print them out as paperback books with covers for families.

Some diaries served as handwritten cookbooks containing recipes created by a particular family cook. For more repair tips on bound diaries-as-cook-books, I recommend the book titled, *How to Wrap a Book*, Fannie Merit Farmer, Boston Cooking School.

How do you repair an old diary or family recipe book to make it more valuable to heirs? You'll often find a bound diary that's torn in the seams. According to my 1990's interview for a magazine article on collecting old and rare cookbooks, with Barbara Gelink, of the Collector's Old Cookbooks Club, San Diego, to repair a book, she reports, you take a bottle of Book Saver Glue (or any other book-repairing or wood glue), and spread the glue along the binder.

Run the glue along the seam and edges. Use wax paper to keep the glue from getting where it shouldn't. Put a heavy glass bottle on the inside page to hold it down while the glue dries.

Use either the *finest* grade sand paper or nail polish remover to unglue tape, tags, or stains from a *glossy* cover. Sit away from heat, light, and sparks. Carefully dampen a terry cloth with nail polish remover, lighter, or cleaning fluid and circle gently until the tag and stain are gone. On a *plastic* book cover, use the finest grade of sandpaper.

Memorabilia such as diaries, genealogy materials, books, photos, ivory, sports trophies, cards, discarded library and school books, or fabrics that end up at estate sales or thrift shops may have adhesive price tags.

To bleach the "discarded book stamp" that libraries and schools often use, or any other rubber stamp mark, price, date, or seals on the pages or edges, use regular bleach, like Clorox. It turns the rubber stamp mark white. The household bleach also turns the edges and pages of the book white as new.

To preserve a valuable, tattered dust jacket with tears along the edges, provide extra firmness. Put a protective plastic wrapper on top of the book jacket cover of a diary, especially if it's handwritten.

Diaries can be bound in colorful, heavy weight print fabrics such as upholstery material and covered by a protective plastic jacket. You have the main ingredient in a time capsule when a diary is placed in a container with memorabilia, genealogy records, surname changes, and DNA test reports for ancestry and/or medical information.

To collect diaries or family photos, look in garage sales, flea markets, and antique shops. Attend auctions and book fairs. Two recommended auction houses for rare cookbooks include Pacific Book Auction Galleries, 139 Townsend, #305, San Francisco, CA 94107, or Sotheby's, New York, 1334 York Ave., New York, NY 10021. Pacific Book Auction Galleries sometimes puts cookbook collections up for an auction.

Look for old high-school graduation class year books to collect from various high schools or middle schools found in garage and estate sales. Restore them and find out whether there's an alumni association whose members want that book stored where all can access it, such as in a public or school library offering interstate library loans.

Can the diary, recipe book, or school yearbook be restored and digitized on DVDs with permission from those who copyrighted it? If you're into keepsake album making with family history photos, diaries, or recipes, look for cookbooks printed by high school parent-teacher associations. Some old ones may be valuable, but even the one put out by the depression era San Diego High School Parent Teacher Association for the class of 1933–34 is only worth $10.

You can start a family history business specializing in restoring diaries, domestic history journals, school yearbooks, and certain types of personal, rare, or cook books. For example, *Cornucopia*, run by Carol A. Greenberg, has old and rare books emphasizing cooking, food literature, domestic history, household management, herbs, kitchen gardens, hotels, restaurants, etiquette, manners, pastimes, amusements, and needlework.

They search for out-of-print books, and are interested in material from the 19th century through 1940. Write to: Little Treasures at PO Box 742, Woodbury, NY 11797. Greenberg is always grateful for quotations on old, rare, and unusual materials in fine condition.

You could start a collector's old diaries and photos club. Marge Rice is a pioneer genealogist who created a hobby of returning heirloom photos to their families of origin. See the related article at: http://www.ancestry.com/library/view/ancmag/7643.asp. Or digitize photos for the Web. See the instructional site on digitizing photos for the Web at: http://www.firstmonday.dk/issues/issue8_1/garner/.

Bound, handwritten diaries originally may have been purchased as blank or lined notebooks. People who collect autographs may also be interested in diaries of authors.

For example, the published diary novel titled: *The Courage to be Jewish and the Wife of an Arab Sheik* is a diary that ended up published as a first person life story, journal, or diary novel spanning three generations. Other diaries end up as cookbooks.

Are diaries worth as much as rare cookbooks? How much are the thousands of rare cookbooks worth today? A helpful guide is the Price Guide to Cookbooks & Recipe Leaflets, 1990, by Linda J. Dickinson, published by Collector Books, at PO Box 3009, Paducah, KY 42002-3009.

See Bibliography of American Cookery Books, 1742-1860. It's based on Waldo Lincoln's American Cookery Books 1742-1860, by Eleanor Lowenstein. Over 800 books and pamphlets are listed. Order from Oak Knoll Books & Press, 414 Delaware St., Newcastle, Delaware 19720.

Louis & Clark Booksellers specialize in rare and out-of-print cookery, gastronomy, wine and beverages, baking, restaurants, domestic history, etiquette, and travel books. They're at 2402 Van Hise Avenue, Madison, WI 53705. Cook books are much more in demand than diaries, unless the author has celebrity status.

Make copies of diaries. Work with the photocopies when you decipher the writing. Store your old diaries in a dry, cool place.

Lining the storage place with plastic that's sealed will keep out vermin, moisture, and bugs. Without moisture, you can keep out the mildew and mold. Store duplicates away from originals. Was something placed in a diary on a certain page, such as a dried rose, letter, farmer's wheat stain, or a special book mark? What meaning did it have?

Look for clues for a time frame. Date the diary. List the date it was begun and when it was ended if you can. List the geographic location of the events in the diary and the writer's travels.

Of what kind of materials is the diary made? Is it improvised, created at low cost by the author? Or is it fancy and belonging to someone of wealth? What is the layout like? Does it show the education of the writer or anything personal? Was it a farmer's almanac, captain's log or sailor's calendar, personal journal or if recent, a Web log (blog)?

What was the writing tool, a quill or a pencil? What's the handwriting like? What century or years? Is it full of details, maps, corsages, and pictures? What is its central message? Do you see patterns or mainly listed facts?

Transcribe the diary with your computer. Read it into a camcorder or on audio tape. It's now oral history. What historical events influenced the writing of the diary? What's the social history? What language is it in or dialect?

Are there vital records such as wills or deeds to real estate mentioned in the diary? Are there directions to a family heirloom or treasure, information in a family Bible, or secret codes and photos?

You've now mended, restored, and conserved a life story and a pattern on the quilt of humanity. Yet nothing compares to Diary time capsules plus DNA test results for family history and ancestry, videos, and other memorabilia.

Diaries and DNA are Evidence

Evidence and diaries: Diaries, like deleted files hidden in the cache pits of computers, and DNA tests can be used as evidence. Diaries also hold the seeds of a story. You could write memoirs, novels or screenplays from diaries and journals.

Diaries also are histories. So preserve a diary as you would restore and preserve a valuable work of art from the past. Diaries are meant to be passed to future generations for a glimpse into a world that can be experienced by generations far into the future.

Keep a file of dates listed in the diary and any objects that surrounded the diary from the same era. Stories with central issues need few explanations. What central issues and themes tell a story in the diaries that cross your path?

Keep the dates and topics organized if you are working with restoring and preserving diaries. There should be a central issue or theme. How old was the person writing the diary? How many years did the individual keep the diary? What kind of objects were near the diary, packed together?

What kind of dust or other stains were on the diary—sawdust? Dog or cat paw prints? Farm materials and plants? The first corsage from the senior prom? Spices? Perfumes? How about recipes, household hints, or how-to tips for hobbies?

Was the diary or journal personal and inner-reflected, or geared toward outer events in the world? Were anecdotes about people and/or pets included, or was it about the feelings of the author of the diary?

Find out what other clues the mystery of the diary unfolds, from the lipstick or nail polish stain to the sawdust and coffee stains, or that faint smell of tobacco, industrial lint, or is it lavender, jasmine or farm dust and straw? Look inside the box in which the diary was packed. It's all evidence and clues waiting to be examined just like a mystery novel. A diary is a story, and everyone life deserves a novel, story, or biography and eventually, a place in a time capsule.

14

Conservation Techniques

How do you rescue and recover memories from mold using conservation techniques? You transport horizontally and store vertically. Store documents and photos in plastic holders, between sheets of waxed paper, or interleave with acid-free paper.

Books are stored spine down. Archive DVDs and CDs in plastic holders and store in plastic crates. To conserve time capsules, according to the American Institute for Conservation of Historic and Artistic Works (AIC), in Washington, DC, neutralize that acid-wracked paper.

Acid Paper:

Use acid-free paper around photos. To store paper that has a high acid content, put the papers in folders and storage boxes with an alkaline reserve to prevent acid migration. Interleave your papers with sheets of alkaline-buffered paper. The buffered paper protects your item from acids that move from areas of high to areas of low concentration. Buffers neutralize acids in paper. A buffer is an alkaline chemical such as calcium carbonate. So you have the choice to use the buffered or non-buffered paper depending on whether your photos are stored against other acid-free materials or printed on acid-free paper.

Photos:

Interweave photos with waxed paper or polyester web covered blotters. Store photos away from overhead water pipes in a cool, dry area with stable humidity and temperatures, not in attics or basements. Keep photos out of direct sunlight and fluorescent lights when on display. Color slides have their own storage requirements.

Keep photos from touching rubber bands, cellophane tape, rubber cement, or paper clips. Poor quality photo paper and paper used in most envelopes and album sleeves also cause photos to deteriorate. Instead, store photos in chemically stable plastic made of polyester, polypropylene, triacetate, or polyethylene. Don't use PCV or vinyl sleeves. Plastic enclosures preserve photos best and keep out the fingerprints and scratches.

Albumen prints are interleaved between groups of photographs. Matte and glossy collodion prints should not be touched by bare hands. Store the same as albumen prints—interleaved between groups of photos.

Silver gelatin printing and developing photo papers are packed in plastic bags inside plastic boxes. Carbon prints and Woodbury prints are packed horizontally. Photomechanical prints are interleaved every two inches and packed in boxes. Transport color photos horizontally—face up.

Chromogenic prints and negatives are packed in plastic bags inside boxes. If you're dealing with cased photos, pack the ambrotypes and pannotypes horizontally in padded containers. Cover the glass of Daguerreotype photos and pack horizontally in padded containers.

Pollutants from the air trapped inside holders and folders destroy photos and paper. Use buffered enclosures for black and white prints and negatives. Use non-buffered paper enclosures to store color prints and color print negatives or cyanotypes and albumen prints.

Store your tintypes horizontally. If you have collodion glass plate negatives, use supports for the glass and binders, and pack horizontally in padded containers. The surface texture of photos stored in plastic can deteriorate. It's called ferrotyping. So don't store negatives in plastic. If you store your photos in paper enclosures, be aware that paper is porous. Instead of plastic or paper storage, put photos in **glass plate negative sleeves in acid-free non-buffered enclosures**.

Then store vertically between pieces of foam board. Where do you find glass plate negative sleeves that can be stored in acid-free non-buffered enclosures? Buy storage materials from companies catering to conservationists, such as *Light Impressions* ®. They're the leading resource for archival supplies. Also look in local craft stores.

Talk to your state archives conservation specialist. Some documents require the work of a trained conservationist. Before you sterilize mold away with bleach, ask your state archives conservationist whether the bleach will ruin your diary or heirloom.

Photo Albums:

Don't make or buy photo albums with "peel-back" plastic over sticky cardboard pieces because they are chemically unstable and could damage anything stored there. Instead, use photo-packet pages made from chemically stable plastic made of polyester, polypropylene, triacetate, or polyethylene. An excellent album would contain archival-quality pages using polyester mounting corners. Acid-free paper mounting corners are next best.

Vellum or Parchment Documents:

Interleave between folders, and pack oversize materials flat. If you have prints and drawings made from chemically stable media, then interleave between folders and pack in cartons. Oversize prints and drawings should be packed in bread trays, or map drawers, placed on poly-covered plywood. Be careful the mildew from plywood doesn't paste onto the back of your print. Look at the poly-covering on the wood.

Take off the frames of your drawings or prints if you can. Books with leather and vellum bindings need to be packed spine down in crates one layer deep. Books and pamphlets should be separated with freezer paper and always packed spine down in crates one layer deep.

Bread trays work well to store parchment and vellum manuscripts that are interleaved between folders. Anything oversize gets packed flat. Posters need to be packed in containers lined with garbage bags because they are *coated* papers. Watercolors and hand-colored prints or inks should be interleaved between folders and packed in crates. Paintings need to be stored *face up* without touching the paint layer. Carry them horizontally.

Computer Tapes and Disks, Audio and Video Tapes:

Store those 'dinosaur' computer tapes in plastic bags packed vertically with plenty of room. Store in plastic crates away from light, heat, or cold. Never touch the magnetic media. If you have an open reel tape, pick up by the hub or reel. Floppy disks should be packed vertically in plastic bags and stored in plastic crates.

With DVDs and CDs, pack vertically in plastic crates and store in plastic drawers or cardboard cartons. Careful—don't touch or scratch the recordable surface. Handle the CD or DVD by the edge. Place audio and video tapes vertically in plastic holders and store them in plastic crates.

Disks made of shellac or acetate and vinyl disks are held by their edges and packed vertically in ethafoam-padded crates. Make sure nothing heavy is placed on CDs, DVDs, tapes, or other disks. You can find ethafoam in most craft stores, or order from a company specializing in storage and presentation tools such as Light Impressions. ®

◆   ◆   ◆

Resources:

American Institute for Conservation
1717 K Street, NW, Suite 200
Washington, DC 20006
tel: 202-452-9545
fax: 202-452-9328
email: info@aic-faic.org
website: http://aic.stanford.edu

Light Impressions (Archival Supplies)
PO Box 22708
Rochester, NY 14692-2708
1-800-828-6216
http://www.lightimpressionsdirect.com

Bibliography:

WAAC Newsletter
http://palimpsest.stanford.edu/aic'disaster
WAAC Newsletter, Vol. 19, No 2 (May, 1997) articles and charts online by Betty Walsh, Conservator, BC Archives, Canada and the Walsh's information at: http://palimpsest.stanford.edu/waac/wn/wn10/wn10-2/wn10-202.html. The site contains material from the WAAC Newsletter, Volume 10, Number 2, May 1988, pp.2-5.

Curatorial Care of Works of Art on Paper, New York: Intermuseum Conservation Association, 1987.

Library Materials Preservation Manual: Practical Methods for Preserving Books, Pamphlets, and Other Printed Materials, Heidi Kyle. 1984

Archives & Manuscripts: Conservation—A Manual on Physical Care and Management, Mary Lynn Ritzenthaler, Society of American Archivists: Chicago, 1993.

Acknowledgement for directions on working with acid-free paper and document recovery tips on packing and water-damaged document rescue is accredited to the resource titled, "Document Recovery Information Packet," Compiled by the California Secretary of State, Archives & Museum Division, 1020 O Street, Sacramento, CA 95814. Their sources include the American Institute for Conservation of Historic and Artistic Works, Washington, DC, and the WAAC Newsletter, Vol. 19, No 2, May, 1997 pp. 12-23, plus chart. Reprinted in "Document Recovery Information Packet," with permission of author, Betty Walsh, Conservator, BC Archives.

15

Launching Life Stories in the Media

Launch your salable life story in the major national press and in various newspapers and magazines of niche markets related to the events in your life, such as weekly newspapers catering to a group: senior citizens, your ethnic group, your local area, or your occupation or area of interest. Your personal history time capsule may be saved to disk and also uploaded to the Web. What about looking for movie deals and book publishers?

If you don't have the money to produce your autobiography as a video biography, or even a film or commercial movie, or publish it for far less cost as a print-on-demand published book, you may wish to find a co-production partner to finance the production of your life story as a cinematic film or made-for-TV video.

At the same time you could contact literary agents and publishers, but one front-page article in a national newspaper or daily newspaper can do wonders to move your life story in front of the gaze of publishers and producers. While you're waiting for a reporter to pay attention to the news angle you have selected for your life story, I highly recommend Michael Wiese's book <u>Film and Video Marketing</u> because it lists some co-production partners as the following:

Private Investors/Consortiums

Foreign Governments (blocked funds)

Financiers

Corporations

Theatrical Distributors

International Theatrical Distributors

International Sales Agents

Home Video

International Home Video

Pay TV

Syndicators

Record Companies

Music Publishers

Book Publishers

Toy Companies

Licensing and Merchandising Firms

Sponsors (products, services)

Public Relations Firms

Marketing Companies/Consultants

Film Bookers

You can also contact actors, directors, producers, feature distributors, home video distributors, entertainment lawyers, brokers, accountants, animation houses, production houses, video post production houses, labs, film facilities, and agents with your script and ask the owners whether they'd be interested in bartering budget items, deferring, or investing in your script.

Private investors could also be professional investors, venture capitalists, and even doctors and dentists who may wish to finance a movie if the potential interests them. You can sell points in your film to investors who finance it as a group of investors, each buying a small percentage of the film for an investment fee.

Or you can approach film investment corporations that specialize in investing in and producing films as partners. They are publicized or listed in the entertainment trade magazines going to producers and workers in the entertainment and film or video industry.

You market your script not only to agents and producers, but to feature distributors, film financiers and co-production partners. This is the first step in finding a way to take your autobiography from script to screen. Learn who distributes what before you approach anyone.

If you want to approach video instead of film, you might wish to know that children's video programming is the fastest-growing genre in original programming. Children's titles account for 10%-15% of the overall home video revenues. According to one of Michael Wiese's books written in the nineties, *Home Video: Producing For The Home Market*, "With retail prices falling and alternative retail outlets expanding, children's programming will soon become one of the most profitable segments of the video market." He was right.

What has happened in the new millennium is that children's program is doing wonderfully. Why? Children's video is repeatable. Children watch the same tape 30 to 50 times. Children's video sells for comparatively lower prices than feature films.

Children's video also rents well. Children's tapes sell it toy stores, book stores, children's stores, and in stores like Woolworth's and Child World. Manufacturers sell tapes at Toy Fair and the American Booksellers Association conventions.

For these reasons, you may wish to write your autobiography as a script for children's video or as a children's book. Video is a burgeoning industry.

According to the market research firm, Fairfield Group, in 1985, the prerecorded video business earned $ 3.3 billion in sales and rentals. This nearly equaled the record and theatrical box office revenues for the same year. The world VCR population is about 100 million. Today we have the DVD and the Internet streaming video.

Back in 1985, the U.S. and Japan accounted for half of the VCRs, followed by the United Kingdom, (9 million) West Germany (nearly 7 million), and Canada, Australia, Turkey, and France (about 3 million each). Spain reported 2 million VCRs. By 1991, the number of VCR ownership increased as prices slowly came down.

Today, in the 21st century, the prerecorded video business has quickly moved to DVD disks, downloadable at a price Internet-based movies, and video tapes are on the way to being a memory of the eighties and early nineties. In the next decade, another media format will be in fashion to replace videos on DVDs and streaming Internet video. The idea is to keep transferring the story from one form of technology to another so that videos made today will be able to be viewed by people in the next century.

The European VCR markets grew faster than in the U.S. during the eighties and nineties just as the DVD markets grew in the early 21st century because there were fewer entertainment alternatives—fewer TV stations, restricted viewing hours, fewer pay TV services, and fewer movie theatres.

You should not overlook the foreign producers for your script. Include Canadian cable T.V., foreign agents, and foreign feature film and video producers among your contacts. Most university libraries open to the public for research include directories listing foreign producers. Photocopy their addresses and send them a query letter and one-page synopsis of your script. Don't overlook the producers from non-English speaking countries. Your script can be translated or dubbed.

You might attend film market type conventions and conferences. They draw producers from a variety of countries. In 1989 at the former Cinetex Film Market in Las Vegas, producers from Canada, Italy, Israel, Spain, and other foreign countries sat next to script writers. All of them were receptive to receiving scripts. They handed one another their business cards. You can learn a lot at summer film markets and film festivals about what kind of scripts are in demand.

Keep a list of which film markets will meet. In the U.S. there are 3 to 5 film markets a year and many more film festivals. Seek out the foreign and local producers with track records and see whether they'd be interested in your script if you have a life story in the form of a script, treatment, or story. Perhaps your theme has some relation to a producer's country or ethnic group. Lots of films are made in Asia, in the Middle East (Israel, Egypt and Tunisia), in Latin America, and Europe or Canada.

Seek out the Australian producers also and New Zealand or India. If you have a low-budget film or home video script set in Korea, Philippines, Japan, or Taiwan, or a specialty film such as Karate or something that appeals to the Indian film market, contact those producers and script agents in those countries. Find out the budget limitations that producers have in the different countries.

Social issues documentaries based on your autobiography are another market for home video. Vestron and other home video distributors use hard-hitting documentaries. Collecting documentary video tapes is like collecting copies of National Geographic magzine. You never throw them out. Tapes are also sold by direct mail. Companies producing and distributing documentaries include MCA, MGM/UA, Vestron, Victory, CBS/Fox, Warner, Media, Karl, Monterey, Thorn/EMI, Embassy, and USA, to name a few.

If you write your autobiography or another's biography as a romance, you might wish to write a script for the video romance series market. Romance video has its roots in the paperback novel. However, the biggest publishers of romance novels have little recognition in retail video stores. Among consumers, publishers of romance novels are popular, but what about to wholesalers and retailers? No. Bookstores, yes. The problem is with pricing. To sell romance videos in bookstores, the tapes would have to be sold at less than $29. In video stores, they can be positioned the same as $59 feature films on video.

Production costs to make high quality romance videos are high. Top stars, top writers, hit book titles, exotic locations, music and special effects are required. Huge volumes of tapes must be sold to break even. Then producers have to search for pay TV, broadcast, or foreign partners. The budget for a one-hour video tape of a thin romance story comes to $500,000.

It's far better to make a low-budget feature film. Romance as a genre has never previously appealed to the video retail buyer. In contrast, a romance paperback sells for a few dollars. Now the question remains: Would women buy a romance-genre video DVD priced at $9.95?

Romance novels successfully have been adapted to audio tape for listening at far less than the cost of video. There is a market for audio scripts of short romance novels and novellas. What is becoming popular today are videos and 'movies' downloadable from the Internet that you can watch on your computer screen or save to a DVD since DVD burners became affordable and popular.

The only way romance videos would work is by putting together a multi-part-nered structure that combines pay TV, home video, book publishing, and domestic and foreign TV. In the eighties, was anyone doing romance video tapes? Yes. Prism Video produced six feature-length romance films, acquired from Comworld. In 1985 the tapes sold for $11.95.

Comworld had limited TV syndication exposure and was one of the first to come out with romance videos. Karl/Lorimar came out with eight romance films from L/A House Productions on a budget of $400,000 each. They were also priced at $11.95 in 1985. To break even, a company has to sell about 60,000 units per title.

Twenty years later, think about researching the romance DVD video and the downloadable Internet video are available field or other genres, especially educational material for various age groups on niche subjects that would appeal to teachers and follow their rules on what is appropriate for their classrooms.

Other media are like open doors to finding a way to put your life story on a disk. Any interview, script, or story can go from print-on-demand published novel or true story book to radio script or stage play.

A video can move from a digital high 8 camcorder with a Firewire 1394 cable attached to a personal computer rapidly into the hard disk drive via Windows XP Movie Maker software. From there it can be saved as a WMV file (a Windows Media file). Then the file can be recorded on a DVD, if long, or a CD if under one hour. Poems can be written, read, and 'burned' to a compact disk (CD) and then mailed out as greeting cards, love letters, or personal histories. Short videos can be emailed.

Romance novels and scripts on audio tape cost less to produce. This market occasionally advertises for romantic novel manuscripts, scripts, and stories in a variety of writer's magazines. Check out the needs of various magazines for journalists and writers online. If you read a lot of romance genre novels or write in this style, you may want to write your autobiography in this genre, but you'd have to market to publishers who use this genre or biographies in other genres such as factual biography.

If your autobiography is set on events which occurred in your childhood, you might prefer to concentrate on writing appropriate for children's video programming. It's a lot easier to sell to the producers who are basking in the current explosion of children's video programming. Perhaps it's your mission to use the video format to teach children.

Will the script of your life story do the following?

teach,

mentor,

motivate,

inspire,

or inform viewers who can be:

children,

teenagers,

parents

or midlifers on their quests for self-identify:

or in their search for facts:

to use as guidelines in making their own decisions:

about life's journeys and writing an introspective journal?

Can your diary be dynamic, dramatic, and empowering to others who may be going through similar stages of life? Are your characters charismatic and memorable, likable and strong?

A life story or autobiography when videotaped or filed as a feature-length movie can spring out of a diary or an inner personal journal (which dialogues with the people who impact your life and observes selected, important events).

Interview Techniques

The events move from the person being interviewed to you, the interviewer, and then into various historical records. In this way you can combine results of DNA testing with actual memories of events. If it's possible, also take notes or have someone take notes in case the tape doesn't pick up sounds clearly.

Keep a backup battery on hand whether you use a tape recorder or a video camera. If at all possible, have a partner bring a spare camera and newly recharged battery. A fully charged battery left overnight has a good chance of going out when you need it.

16

DNA-Driven Genealogy

According to monthly newsletters from Family Tree DNA, ([http://www.](http://www.familytreedna.com)
[familytreedna.com](http://www.familytreedna.com)) and their *Facts & Genes* newsletter, November 21, 2002 Volume 1, Issue 5, you can find out what percentage of the US population holds your surname by going to the US Government census site at: http://www. census.gov/genealogy/www/freqnames.html. The site also covers the methodology that the Census Bureau used to come up with the percentages and rank for the surnames.

The US population on April 1, 2000 was 281,421,906 people. If you would like a rough idea of the males with your surname in the US, first search the site <http://www.census.gov/genealogy/www/freqnames.html> to get the percentage for your surname. Multiply that percentage times the population of the 2000 census. In their rough calculation, they will assume that 50% are males, so now divide by 2. This is an estimate of the number of males with your surname. To estimate the number of adult males, multiply by .7. The formula is:
Percentage * 281,421,906/ 2 * .7 = adult males with surname

You can also find out how common your surname is in the UK at the site: http://www.taliesin-arlein.net/names/search.php. There are 269,353 surnames in the UK database, representing 54,412,638 people. This database is provided by the Office of National Statistics of the UK, and gives an actual count of the number of persons for each surname. Their database is an extract of an Office of National Statistics database, and provides a list of surnames in use in England, Wales and the Isle of Mann in September 2002.

The US Census population database and the Office of National Statistics of the UK database used different methodologies to come up with their results. Rare surnames will not get a search result in the US census site, whereas they will in the UK site, even if there are only a few persons with the same surname. Names shared by fewer than five people have been excluded from the UK list.

Now that you have an idea of the size of your potential prospect pool, lets assume that only 1/3 are interested in genealogy, so you now divide by 3. The end result is a very rough approximation of the number of potential participants available. If you are only using the Internet to find your participants, cut this number in half for the US. Other countries have a smaller percentage of persons on the Internet than the US.

As your first step, you have probably posted your project to as many sites and mailing lists that are applicable and allow such postings. You have probably also put up a web site, even if it is only one page. Most likely you have contacted all those persons whom you had contact with in the past regarding genealogy. Here are some suggestions to make more people aware of your project:

1. Consult the Directory of Family Associations. If there is a Family Association for your surname, contact them and offer to write an article for their publication about your project.

2. Register your web site with familysearch.org. Everyone searching on your surname at Familysearch.org will find your web site. You must first register yourself with familysearch.org to be able to submit your website for consideration.

3. Visit your local Family History Center, and offer to show the Genealogy by Genetics video to the staff and patrons. This might not find you any participants, but if every Group Administrator takes an hour to do this, then all the Surname Projects might find participants.

4. Review your web site. It needs to be easy to understand for those not familiar with DNA testing, and clearly present the benefits to the participant. What will they gain from participating? How will it help them in their research? What might the results tell them?

5. Find out if there are any genealogy clubs or organizations in your area, and volunteer to show the video, and answer questions.

DNA testing for genealogy is a new field, and we are all pioneers. Most likely you have learned a lot about the field as a result of your testing. Those of us who have learned about DNA testing and how to interpret the results are aware of the benefits and how the testing can assist us with our genealogy research.

The majority of those interested in Family History research most likely aren't aware of Genetic Genealogy. If you volunteer an hour to help your fellow genealogists understand this new tool, and help more people become knowledgeable, all of us will benefit as we seek participants for our testing. Look for social histories of the ethnic group you're researching.

When you're working with DNA, you can look for historical medical records. Only a few are open to the public. You might try the microfilmed collections at The Family History Library in Salt Lake City, UT, or rent one of the microfilms from any of the worldwide family history centers, usually found in a genealogical library in various cities around the world.

Look at records from the Eugenics Record Office (ERO) that operated from 1910 to 1944. The purpose of that office was to study human genetics in order to reduce inheritable genetic disorders. You can look over the 520 rolls of microfilm. Visit the Family History Library Catalog and look under United States—Medical Records—Eugenics.

Look up the state you want, and look under Medical Records. You might want to read up on the controversial Eugenics movement. Think about how DNA testing today differs in that the test results are used today either to find relatives, ancestors, or tailor individual therapies for individual genetic make-ups—phenomics.

How times have changed. Or have they? What do you see in your own DNA and family history research? The Family History Library in Salt Lake City also has some historical hospital records.

One example is the Northwestern Memorial Hospital record, Chicago in the Family History Library, dated 1896-1933. Perhaps one of your relatives is in those files. That's one other way of finding a maiden name from the days when many people were never given a birth certificate because they were born at home and never registered. That's what happened with my mom, born in 1904 at home in NY state.

Understanding your Results: Ethnic Origin

Whether you are just starting a **Surname Project**, or ordered a test to learn about DNA testing for genealogy, everyone experiences the situation of receiving the first test result, and what now? You have one test result, and what do you do with a string of 12 or 25 numbers? Can they tell you anything? Where can you find the information you need?

In the situation of the one or first test result, most likely you will not find others to whom you are related. The odds of a random match to some one to whom you are related when you are the first of your surname to test is slim to none. Instead, you might find some clues to your ethnic origin.

To find clues about your ethnic origin, Log into FamilyTreeDna.com, and at your Personal Page click on Recent Ethnic Origins to search this data base. The results show others whom you match, or who are a near match, and their ancestor's ethnic origin.

The information on their ethnic origin is provided by each person tested (testee). The information provided for ethnic origin is only as accurate as the knowledge held by the testee regarding their ancestors.

Testees are instructed to answer unknown for ethnic origin when their ancestor's origin is not known, or not certain. Sometimes the origin the testees provided is incorrect.

Incorrect origins provided by testees may lead to search results that do not seem logical. For example: Assume your ancestors are from England, but your search results show the ethnic origin of your matches as England, France, AND one match shows an origin of Native American. Does that mean that your ancestor's relatives may have lived in England and France? Yes.

Does it mean that your ancestor was also a Native American? No. It means that a settler in America had a child with a Native American woman, the child was brought up as a Native American, and that, over time, the family has "forgotten" the European ancestor, and believes their ancestry to be Native American.

During the span of generations people tend to move, as do borders, so nationality or ethnicity becomes subjective. For example, testees may enter Germany for ethnic origin, because the land of their ancestors is in Germany today, but the land had been held by Denmark for many centuries.

Your search should return at least one match, namely yourself. If your results show 3 matches from Ireland and 1 from Scotland, and you have reported to us that your ancestors came from Scotland, then you are the Scotland result. The other 3 matches are either from the Family Tree DNA database or from the databases Family Tree DNA have been supplied by the University of Arizona.

To see how your ethnic origin is recorded in our database, click on the link titled Update Contact Information. You can also update your paternal and maternal ethnic origin on this Update Contact Information page.

Exact matches show people who are the closest to you genetically. The Ethnic origin shows where they have been reported to have lived. Since many persons migrated since the beginning of time, you will typically see matches in more than one country.

For information purposes, the Recent Ethnic Origin search also displays results for those who are not exact matches, but are 'near matches'. A near match is either one step or two steps from your result. An exact match is 12/12 or 25/25. A one step match is 11/12 or 24/25. A two step match is 10/12 or 23/25. The value of the near matches is to see where those who may be related migrated over time.

Other databases available that you can search are:

European: http://ystr.charite.de/index_gr.html

US: http://www.ystr.org/usa/

In some cases you will not find any results. This is because only a very small percentage of the world population has been tested and is in the databases. The Ystr databases, plus the FamilyTreeDNA Recent Ethnic Origin database together hold about 21,000 test results. Every day more results are added, and it is only a matter of time before you will have some matches. Your test with Family Tree DNA includes access to our databases for matching.

If you do not find any results in the two YSTR databases shown above, try entering your result, and then eliminating a marker, and do this until you have a smaller set of markers that results in some matches. This might provide some clues regarding where your markers have occurred geographically. The value of DNA testing comes from comparing your results to others. If you have started a Surname Project, you will most likely have results from others soon. If you only tested yourself, you may want to consider either using DNA testing to solve one of your Family History questions, or starting a Surname Project.

Haplotypes: Convergence

A Haplotype is the 12 Marker result from testing the Y chromosome. Some Haplotypes are common, with a high frequency of occurrence and some Haplotypes are rare, with a low frequency of occurrence.

Many people have common Haplotypes, which means that they would expect to find matches to those who do not have their surname. This occurs because we were all at one point related. As the different branches of the Adam +Eve tree evolved throughout time, mutations occurred, forming different Haplotypes.

Thousands of years later, you have many different Haplotypes. Due to these mutations, you could have two branches that mutate to an identical Haplotype. This is called convergence. If your Haplotype matches an individual with a different surname, and your genealogy research shows no evidence of an extra-marital event or adoption, your match may be the result of Convergence.

The example below shows convergence between the ABC surname and the XYZ surname, using just 3 markers to keep the example simple. Notice how the mutations over time bring two different Family Lines to the point that they match.

Time	ABC	XYZ
1000 A.D.	12 24 15	14 25 13
1200	13 24 15	14 25 13
1400	13 24 15	14 25 14
1600	13 24 15	14 24 14
1800	13 24 15	13 24 14
2000	13 24 14	13 24 14

Convergence explains why a haplotype will match others with a different surname. DNA testing for genealogy is not a substitute for genealogy research, but is instead a companion. Results that match must be considered in light of the genealogy research. If you match someone with a different surname, most likely there wasn't an adoption or extra marital event, and your match may be the result of convergence.

Case Studies in Genetic Genealogy

In each issue of the Newsletter, Family Tree DNA looks at what Genetic Genealogy will do for your Family History research. This article is a continuation of the topic, with situations, called "*Case Studies*", followed by a recommendation. The objective of the case studies is to present different situations you may encounter in your family history research, and how DNA testing can be applied.

Case Study

From November 21, 2002 Volume 1, Issue 5, *Family Tree DNA Newsletter*, "I have participated in a Surname Project, and had quite surprising results. All the other Lines of my surname are related, except my Line. We have all traced our ancestors to England. Not only is my line not related, but also my ethnic origin is Eastern European. What do I do now?"

Recommendation

From November 21, 2002 Volume 1, Issue 5, *Family Tree DNA Newsletter*, "I am sure you were quite surprised, and perhaps disappointed. The first step is to validate the result for your Line or family tree. Since only one person was tested for your Line, we recommend testing additional males from each branch on your tree, to see if they all match each other. If they end up matching, your result is probably due to an extra marital event, an adoption, or a name or spelling change.

"In reviewing the surnames of Eastern Europe, your surname is pronounced as the surname in England, only the spelling is different. A review of your Family History shows that the research and documentation for the time period 1800–1850 is quite sparse. Many more records are available in England for this time period, including parish registers and wills. I would suggest that more family history research might shed some light on the situation."

Managing a Genetic Genealogy Project: Participants with Poor Documentation

Occasionally you might run across a willing participant for your Surname Project who has a poorly documented family tree, perhaps even built entirely out of the International Genealogical Index (IGI) by matching surnames. Your dilemma is that the prospective participant appears to be from a Line you haven't tested yet, but without better research you can't be sure. What comes first, the testing or the research?

This is a complex issue. If you turn away the participant and suggest that they do more research, they may become discouraged, and never return. If the participant tests, and gets unexpected results, they may become an unhappy participant.

One solution is to fill in the gaps of their research. You may not have the time to take this step. A better solution may be to communicate the situation to the participant, and let them make the decision to test now with the possibility of unexpected results, and also encourage them to do further research.

Perhaps from your research experience, you may be able to suggest to the participant specific sources for them to investigate. Most likely, they want to do more research, and just need some guidance and direction.

It will be a win-win for both the Surname Project and the participant if you are able to achieve both additional research on their part, and their participation.

If you're interested in receiving Facts & Genes newsletter, feel free to contact the editor at Family Tree DNA with your comments, feedback, questions to be addressed, as well as suggestions for future articles. If you would like your Surname Project featured in their *Spotlight* column in a future issue, please send an email telling them about your project. If you are a Project Manager and can help others with tips or suggestions, please contact the editor: editor@ familytreedna.com.

17

Greek Genealogy

Greek Genealogy is a world-shaper unto itself with videos, publications, and rich oral history. Everybody becomes Greek for a day at Greek music and food festivals. At one Greek genealogy Web site at: http://www.daddezio.com/catalog/grkndx20.html, you'll learn that name days instead of birthdays are celebrated in Greece according to "fairly rigid conventions."

The Internet has numerous Greek genealogy Web sites, some helping to reunite numerous adoptees with their original families through genealogy research. To start your Greek genealogy search, I highly recommend the book titled, A History of the Greeks in the Americas 1453-1938. You can find it online at Amazon.com at the Web site: http://www.amazon.com/exec/obidos/ASIN/1882792157/. You'll find an excellent publication on Greek genealogy titled: Greek Genealogy Publications by Lica H. Catsakis at the Web site: http://www.feefhs.org/misc/pub-lhc.html.

Also I highly recommend these books on Greek genealogy:

The Greeks in America
http://www.amazon.com/exec/obidos/ASIN/0822510103/

The Family in Greek History
http://www.amazon.com/exec/obidos/ASIN/0674292707/

Check out these Greek genealogy Web sites:

goGreece.com: Genealogy
http://gogreece.com/society_culture/genealogy.html

Hellenes-Diaspora Greek Genealogy
http://www.geocities.com/SouthBeach/Cove/4537/Main1.html

• Begin your genealogy search with maps of your ancestor's town, city, and neighborhood. For example, you'll find an excellent source with *Greek Genealogy Research, 2nd Edition* (1993), 82 pages, with assistance from Dan Schlyter, and *Greek Gazetteer, Volume 1* (1997), 120 pages, by Lica Catsakis.

It's easier to find information on searching Greek genealogy than in some of the other countries of Eastern Europe and the Middle East that formerly were under the Ottoman Empire, except where fire destroyed records as it did in parts of Crete. At the Web site titled "Greece.com Society and Culture" at http:// gogreece.com/society_culture/genealogy.html, you'll find "an extensive collection of links to web sites relevant to genealogical research, as well as, mailing lists, and articles relevant to Greek culture."

What's great about this Web site is that contains a description and list of the Greek genealogy sites. Also try the message board at: GreekFamilies.com at: http://www.greekfamilies.com/pages/138257/index.htm. Look at the Hellenic Genealogy Web site at: http://www.geocities.com/SouthBeach/Cove/4537/. Also, you'll find excellent Web sites on Greek (Hellenic) genealogy at Dimitri's Surname Database at: http://www.dimitri.8m.com/surnames.html. You can search many Greek surnames there and their ancestral origins. For example, my mother's brother's daughter's Greek surname, Fotiadis comes from Thessalonikis in Macedonia. So to look up the origin, I'd have to realize that the variant spellings of Photiadis and Fotiadis are variations of the same name and that I should look in the "F" and the "P" files. On this surname database, it's listed under "F."

If you're ancestors are Greek, chances are you've kept in contact with other Greek family members, unless you're an adoptee or come from a family that has intermarried several generations back. Then here's your chance to get in touch again. Go to the Greek Roots Center at: http://www.butterbox.gr/. Roots Research Center is a non-profit, voluntary, non governmental organization, helping adults adoptees with Greek roots to discover their origins.

The Roots Research Center has information on orphanages in Greece. Write to them at: Roots Research Center, P.O Box 71514, Vyron, 16210, Athens,Greece. They cooperate with all Founding houses of Greece, Red Cross reunion section, International Social Service Greek section, Hellenes Diasporas and every other willing Organization and offer "an independent mediation service where prospective adoptive parts, birth relatives can be helped to make cooperative arrangements about contact."

There are many Greek children who were adopted by families in many different countries, including the USA. Some of them don't have written records or adoption files. If you want to meet your birth family or find out more about your Greek roots, you should know that some Greek families who want to find descendants of adopted children can't find missing members because they can't afford to pay for research in other nations. If this is your genealogy research project, feel free to contact the Roots Research Center at: 56 PANEPISTIMIOU STR 104 31, in Athens, or at their Confidential Address, P.O Box 71514, 16210 Gr.

APPENDIX A

General Genealogy Web sites

Ancestry.com: http://www.ancestry.com/main.htm?lfl=m

Cyndi's List of Genealogy on the Internet: http://www.cyndislist.com/

Cyndi's List is a categorized & cross-referenced index to genealogical resources on the Internet with thousands of links.

DistantCousin.com (Uniting Cousins Worldwide) http://distantcousin.com/ Links/surname.html

Ellis Island Online: http://www.ellisisland.org/

Family History Library: http://www.familysearch.org/Eng/default.asp

http://www.familysearch.org/Eng/Search/frameset_search.asp

(The Church of Jesus Christ of Latter Day Saints) International Genealogical Index Female Ancestors: http://www.cyndislist.com/female.htm

Genealogist's Index to the Web: http://www.genealogytoday.com/GIWWW/?

Genealogy Web http://www.genealogyweb.com/

Genealogy Authors and Speakers: http://feefhs.org/frg/frg-a&l.html

Genealogy Today: http://www.genealogytoday.com/

My Genealogy.com: http://www.genealogy.com/cgi-bin/my_main.cgi

Scriver, Dr. Charles: The Canadian Medical Hall of Fame http://www.virtualmuseum.ca/Exhibitions/Medicentre/en/scri_print.htm

Surname Sites: http://www.cyndislist.com/surn-gen.htm

National Genealogical Society: http://www.ngsgenealogy.org/index.htm

United States List of Local by State Genealogical Societies: http://www.
daddezio.com/society/hill/index.html

United States Vital Records List: http://www.daddezio.com/records/room/
index.html or http://www.cyndislist.com/usvital.htm

Appendix B

Web Resources on Former Ottoman Empire Genealogy Web Sites

Albanian Research List: http://feefhs.org/al/alrl.html

Armenian Genealogical Society: http://feefhs.org/am/frg-amgs.html

Egyptian Genealogy: http://www.daddezio.com/egypgen.html

Egyptian Genealogy—Kindred Trails (tm): http://www.kindredtrails.com/egypt.html

Egyptian Royal Genealogy: http://www.geocities.com/christopherjbennett/

Historical Society of Jews from Egypt http://www.hsje.org/homepage.htm

Jewish Genealogy: http://www.jewishgen.org/infofiles/

Lebanon Genealogy http://genforum.genealogy.com/lebanon

http://www.mit.edu:8001/activities/lebanon/map.html

Lebanese descendants of the Bourjaily Family (Abou R'Jaily) http://www.abourjeily.com/Family/index.htm
Descendants of Atallah Abou Rjeily, born about 1712

Lebanese Club of New York City:
http://nyc.lebaneseclub.org/
http://www.rootsweb.com/~lbnwgw/lebclubnyc/index.htm

Lebanese Genealogy: http://www.rootsweb.com/~lbnwgw/

Middle East Genealogy: http://www.rootsweb.com/~mdeastgw/index.html

Middle East Genealogy by country: http://www.rootsweb.com/~mdeastgw/ index.html#country

Sephardim.com: http://www.sephardim.com/

Syrian and Lebanese Genealogy: http://www.genealogytoday. com/family/syrian/

Syria Genealogy: http://www.rootsweb.com/~syrwgw/

Syrian/Lebanese/Jewish/Farhi Genealogy Site (Flowers of the Orient) http://www.farhi.org

Turkish Genealogy Discussion Group: http://www.turkey. com/forums/forumdisplay.php3?forumid=18

Turkish Telephone Directories Information: Türk Telekomünikasyon (Tele-communication) http://ttrehber.gov.tr/rehber_webtech/index.asp

Croatia Genealogy Cross Index: http://feefhs.org/cro/indexcro.html

Eastern Europe: http://www.cyndislist.com/easteuro.htm

Eastern European Genealogical Society, Inc.: http://feefhs.org/ca/frg-eegs.html

Eastern Europe Index: http://feefhs.org/ethnic.html

Egyptian Genealogy: http://www.kindredtrails.com/egypt.html

India Royalty: http://freepages.genealogy.rootsweb.com/~royalty/india/ persons.html

Romanian American Heritage Center: http://feefhs.org/ro/frg-rahc.html

Slavs, South: Cultural Society: http://feefhs.org/frg-csss.html

Ukrainian Genealogical and Historical Society of Canada: http://feefhs.org/ca/frgughsc.html

Rom (Gypsies): http://www.cyndislist.com/peoples.htm#Gypsies

APPENDIX C

Bibliography 1.

Genealogy:

A Bintel Brief: Sixty Years of Letters From the Lower East Side to the Jewish Daily Forward. Metzker, Isaac, ed Doubleday and Co. 1971. Garden City, NY
Climbing Your Family Tree: Online and Offline Genealogy for Kids IRA Wolfman, Tim Robinson (Illustrator), Alex Haley (Introduction)/ Paperback/ Workman Publishing Company, Inc./ October 2001

Complete Beginner's Guide to Genealogy, the Internet, and Your Genealogy Computer Program Karen Clifford/ Paperback/ Genealogical Publishing Company, Incorporated/ February 2001

Complete Idiot's Guide(R) to Online Geneology Rhonda McClure/ Paperback/ Pearson Education/ January 2002

Creating Your Family Heritage Scrapbook : From Ancestors to Grandchildren, Your Complete Resource & Idea Book for Creating a Treasured Heirloom. Nerius, Maria Given, Bill Gardner ISBN: 0761530142 Published by Prima Publishing, Aug 2001

Cyndi's List: A Comprehensive List of 70,000 Genealogy Sites on the Internet (Vol. 1 & 2) Cyndi Howells/ Paperback/ Genealogical Publishing Company, Incorporated/ June 2001.

Discovering Your Female Ancestors: Special strategies for uncovering your hard-to-find information about your female lineage. Carmack, Sharon DeBartolo. Conference Lecture on Audio Tape: Carmack, Sharon DeBartolo.

Folklife and Fieldwork: A Layman's Introduction to Field Techniques. Bartis, Peter. Washington, DC: Library of Congress, 1990.

Genealogy Online for Dummies Matthew L. Helm, April Leigh Helm, April Leigh Helm, Matthew L. Helm/ Paperback/ Wiley, John & Sons, Incorporated/ February 2001

Genealogy Online Elizabeth Powell Crowe/ Paperback/ McGraw-Hill Companies, November 2001

History From Below: How to Uncover and Tell the Story of Your Community, Association, or Union. Brecher, Jeremy. New Haven: Advocate Press/ Commonwork Pamphlets, 1988.

My Family Tree Workbook: Genealogy for Beginners Rosemary A. Chorzempa/ Paperback/ Dover Publications, Incorporated/

National Genealogical Society Quarterly 79, no. 3 (September 19991): 183-93

"**Numbering Your Genealogy: Sound and Simple Systems**." Curran, Joan Ferris.

Oral History and the Law. Neuenschwander, John. Pamphlet Series #1. Albuquerque: Oral History Association, 1993.

Oral History for the Local Historical Society. Baum, Willa K. Nashville: American Association for State and Local History, 1987.

Scrapbook Storytelling: Save Family Stories & Memories with Photos, Journaling & Your Own Creativity Slan, Joanna Campbell, Published by EFG, Incorporated, ISBN: 0963022288 May 1999

"**The Silent Woman: Bringing a Name to Life**." NE-59. Boston, MA: New England Historic Genealogical Society Sesquicentennial Conference, 1995.

The Source: A Guidebook of American Genealogy Alice Eichholz, Loretto Dennis Szucs (Editor), Sandra Hargreaves Luebking (Editor), Sandra Hargreaves Luebking (Editor)/ Hardcover/ MyFamily.com, Incorporated/ February 1997

To Our Children's Children: Journal of Family Members, Bob Greene, D. G. Fulford 240pp. ISBN: 038549064X Publisher: Doubleday & Company, Incorporated: October 1998.

Transcribing and Editing Oral History. Nashville: American Association for State and Local History, 1991.

Using Oral History in Community History Projects. Buckendorf, Madeline, and Laurie Mercier. Pamphlet Series #4. Albuqueque: Oral History Association, 1992.

Unpuzzling Your Past: The Best-Selling Basic Guide to Genealogy (Expanded, Updated and Revised) Emily Anne Croom, Emily Croom/ Paperback/ F & W Publications, Incorporated/ August 2001

Writing a Woman's Life. Heilbrun, Carolyn G. New York: W.W. Norton, 1988

Your Guide to the Family History Library: How to Access the World's Largest Genealogy Resource Paula Stuart Warren, James W. Warren/ Paperback/ F & W Publications, Incorporated/ August 2001

Your Story:
A Guided Interview Through Your Personal and Family History, 2nd ed., 64pp.ISBN: 0966604105 Publisher: Stack Resources, LLC

APPENDIX D

Bibliography 2.

Genealogy in the Former Ottoman Empire

See: <u>McGowan, Bruce William, 1933-</u> **Defter-i mufassal-i liva-i Sirem : an Ottoman revenue survey dating from the reign of Selim II./ Bruce William McGowan.**
Ann Arbor, Mich.: University Microfilms, 1967.
See: **Bogaziçi University** Library Web sites:
<u>http://seyhan.library.boun.edu.tr/search/wN{232}ufus+Defter/</u>
<u>wN{232}ufus+Defter/1,29,29,B/frameset&FF=wN{232}ufus+Defter&9,9</u>,
or <u>http://seyhan.library.boun.edu.tr/search/dTaxation+—+Turkey.</u>
<u>/dtaxation+turkey/-5,-1,0,B/exact&FF=dtaxation+turkey&1,57</u>,
Jurisdictions and localities in Bulgaria:
Michev N. and P. Koledarov. *Rechnik na selishchata i selishchnite imena v Bulgariia, 1878–1987* (Dictionary of villages and village names in Bulgaria, 1878–1987), Sofia: Nauka i izkustvo, 1989 (FHL book 949.77 E5m).

See: <u>McGowan, Bruce William, 1933-</u> **Defter-i mufassal-i liva-i Sirem : an Ottoman revenue survey dating from the reign of Selim II./ Bruce William McGowan.**
Ann Arbor, Mich.: University Microfilms, 1967.

Web sites Research and Genealogy in the Former Ottoman Empire

See: **Bogaziçi University** Library Web sites:
<u>http://seyhan.library.boun.edu.tr/search/wN{232}ufus+Defter/</u>
<u>wN{232}ufus+Defter/1,29,29,B/frameset&FF=wN{232}ufus+Defter&9,9</u>,

or <u>http://seyhan.library.boun.edu.tr/search/dTaxation+—+Turkey.</u>
<u>/dtaxation+turkey/-5,-1,0,B/exact&FF=dtaxation+turkey&1,57</u>,

APPENDIX E

Bibliography 3.

DNA Testing and Genetics

A Biologist's Guide to Analysis of DNA Microarray Data Steen Knudsen/ Hardcover/ Wiley, John & Sons, Incorporated/ April 2002

Advances and Opportunities in DNA Testing and Gene Probes Business Communications Company Incorporated (Editor)/ Hardcover/ Business Communications/ September 1996

African Exodus, The Origins of Modern Humanity Stringer, Christopher and Robin McKie. Henry Holt And Company 1997

An A to Z of DNA Science: What Scientists Mean when They Talk about Genes and Genomes Jeffre L. Witherly, Galen P. Perry, Darryl L. Leja/ Paperback/ Cold Spring Harbor Laboratory Press/ September 2002

An Introduction to Forensic DNA Analysis Norah Rudin, Keith Inman/ Hardcover/ CRC Press/ December 2001

Archaeogenetics: DNA and the population prehistory of Europe, Ed. Colin Renfrew & Katie Boyle. McDonald Institute Monographs. Cambridge, UK, Distributed by Oxbow Books UK. In USA: The David Brown Book Company, Oakville, CT. 2000

Cartoon Guide to Genetics Gonick, Larry, With Mark Wheelis: Paperback/ HarperInformation/ July 1991

DNA Detectives, The—Working Against Time, novel, Hart, Anne. Mystery and Suspense Press, iuniverse.com paperback 248 pages at http://www.iuniverse.com or 1-877-823-9235.

DNA for Family Historians (ISBN 0-9539171-0-X). Savin, Alan of Maidenhead, England, is author of the 32-page book. See the Web site: http://www.savin.org/dna/dna-book.html

DNA Microarrays and Gene Expression Pierre Baldi, G. Wesley Hatfield, G. Wesley Hatfield/ Hardcover/ Cambridge University Press/ August 2002

Microarrays for an Integrative Genomics Isaac S. Kohane, Alvin Kho, Atul J. Butte/ Hardcover/ MIT Press/ August 2002

Does It Run in the Family?: A Consumers Guide to DNA Testing for Genetic Disorders Doris Teichler Zallen, Doris Teichler-Zallen, Doris Teichler Zallen/ Hardcover/ Rutgers University Press/ May 1997

Double Helix, The: A Personal Account of the Discovery of the Structure of DNA James D. Watson/ Paperback/ Simon & Schuster Trade Paperbacks/ June 2001

Genes, Peoples, and Languages Luigi Luca Cavalli-Sforza, Mark Seielstad (Translator).

Genetic Witness: Forensic Uses of DNA Tests DIANE Publishing Company (Editor)/ Paperback/ DIANE Publishing Company/ April 1993

History and Geography of Human Genes, The [ABRIDGED] L. Luca Cavalli-Sforza, Paolo Menozzi (Contributor), Alberto Piazza (Contributor).

How to DNA Test Our Family Relationships Terry Carmichael, Alexander Ivanof Kuklin, Ed Grotjan/ Paperback/ Acen Press/ November 2000

Introduction to Genetic Analysis Anthony J. Griffiths, Suzuki, Lewontin, Gelbart, David T. Suzuki, Richard C. Lewontin, Willi Gelbart, Miller, Jeffrey H. Miller/ Hardcover/ W. H. Freeman Company/ February 2000

Jefferson's Children: The Story of One American Family Shannon Lanier, Jane Feldman, Lucian K. Truscott (Introduction)/ Hardcover/ Random House Books for Young Readers/ September 2000

Medical Genetics Lynn B. B. Jorde, Michael J. Bamshad, Raymond L. White, Michael J. Bamshad, John C. Carey, John C. Carey, Raymond L. White, John C. Carey/ Paperback/ Mosby-Year Book, Inc./ July 2000

Molecule Hunt, The: Archaeology and the Search for Ancient DNA Martin Jones/ Hardcover/ Arcade/ April 2002

More Chemistry and Crime: From Marsh Arsenic Test to DNA Profile Richard Saferstein, Samuel M. Gerber (Editor)/ Hardcover/ American Chemical Society/ August 1998

1996, Quest For Perfection—The Drive to Breed Better Human Beings, Maranto, Gina. Scribner, 1996

Our Molecular Future: How Nanotechnology, Robotics, Genetics, and Artificial Intelligence Will Transform Our World Mulhall, Douglas./ Hardcover/ Prometheus Books/ March 2002

Paternity—Disputed, Typing, PCR and DNA Tests: Index of New Information Dexter Z. Franklin/ Hardcover/ Abbe Pub Assn of Washington Dc/ January 1998

Paternity in Primates: Tests and Theories R. D. Martin (Editor), A. F. Dickson (Editor), E. J. Wickings (Editor)/ Hardcover/ Karger, S Publishers/ December 1991

Queen Victoria's Gene: Hemophilia and the Royal Family (Pbk) D. M. Potts, W. T. Potts/ Paperback/ Sutton Publishing, Limited/ June 1999

Redesigning Humans: Our Inevitable Genetic Future Stock, Gregory./ Hardcover/ Houghton Mifflin Company/ April 2002

Rosalind Franklin: The Dark Lady of DNA, Brenda Maddox/ Hardcover/ HarperCollins Publishers/ October 2002

Schaum's Outline Of Genetics Susan Elrod, William D. Stansfield/ Paperback/ McGraw-Hill Companies, The/ December 2001

Seven Daughters of Eve, The: The Science That Reveals Our Genetic Ancestry. Sykes, Bryan. **ISBN:** 0393323145 **Publisher:** Norton, W. W. & Company, Inc. May 2002

Stedman's OB-GYN & Genetics Words Ellen Atwood (Editor), Stedmans/ Paperback/ Lippincott Williams & Wilkins/ December 2000

APPENDIX F

Middle East Genealogy Books

Before Taliban: Genealogies of the Afghan Jihad
by David B. Edwards (**Paperback**—April 2002)

Nationalism and the Genealogical Imagination: Oral History and Textual Authority in Tribal Jordan (Comparative Studies on Muslim Societies ; 23)
by Andrew Shryock (**Paperback**—February 1997)

Old Bohemian and Moravian Jewish Cemeteries
by Arno Parik, et al

Al-Sabah: Genealogy and History of Kuwait's Ruling Family, 1752-1986 (Middle East Cultures Series, No 13)
by Alan Rush

Genealogies of Conflict: Class, Identity, and State in Palestine/Israel and South Africa
by Ran Greenstein

History of Seyd Said, Sultan of Muscat
by Shaik Mansur, Robin Bidewell (Introduction) (**Hardcover**—1984)

Amarna Personal Names (American Schools of Oriental Research Dissertation, Vol 9)
by Richard S. Hess (**Hardcover**—October 1996)

Soberanos de leyenda
by Antonio García Jiménez

◆   ◆   ◆

Iran Genealogy-Related Books

Another Sea, Another Shore: Stories of Iranian Migration
by Shouleh Vatanabadi, et all (2003)

Funny in Farsi: A Memoir of Growing Up Iranian in America
by Firoozeh Dumas (2003)

Wedding Song: Memoirs of an Iranian Jewish Woman
by Farideh Goldin (2003)

Exiled Memories: Stories of the Iranian Diaspora
by Zohreh Sullivan (2001)

Journey from the Land of No : A Girlhood Caught in Revolutionary Iran
by Roya Hakakian (2004)

Inside Iran: Women's Lives
by Jane Mary Howard (2002)

APPENDIX G

List of Published Paperback Books in Print Written by Anne Hart

Title: Writer's Guide to Book Proposals: Templates, Query Letters, & Free Media Publicity
ISBN: 0-595-31673-5

Title: How to Interpret Family History and Ancestry DNA Test Results for Beginners: The Geography and History of Your Relatives
ISBN: 0-595-31684-0

Title: Cover Letters, Follow-Ups, and Book Proposals: Samples with Templates
ISBN: 0-595-31663-8

Title: How to Make Money Organizing Information
ISBN: 0-595-23695-2

Title: How To Stop Elderly Abuse: A Prevention Guidebook
ISBN: 0-595-23550-6

Title: How to Make Money Teaching Online With Your Camcorder and PC: 25 Practical and Creative How-To Start-Ups To Teach Online
ISBN: 0-595-22123-8

Title: A Private Eye Called Mama Africa: What's an Egyptian Jewish Female Psycho-Sleuth Doing Fighting Hate Crimes in California?
ISBN: 0-595-18940-7

Title: The Freelance Writer's E-Publishing Guidebook: 25+ E-Publishing Home-based Online Writing Businesses to Start for Freelancers
ISBN: 0-595-18952-0

Title: The Courage to Be Jewish and the Wife of an Arab Sheik: What's a Jewish Girl from Brooklyn Doing Living as a Bedouin?
ISBN: 0-595-18790-0

Title: Power Dating Games: What's Important to Know About the Person You'll Marry
ISBN: 0-595-19186-X

Title: Four Astronauts and a Kitten: A Mother and Daughter Astronaut Team, the Teen Twin Sons, and Patches, the Kitten: The Intergalactic Friendship Club
ISBN: 0-595-19202-5

Title: The Writer's Bible: Digital and Print Media: Skills, Promotion, and Marketing for Novelists, Playwrights, and Script Writers. Writing Entertainment Content for the New and Print Media.
ISBN: 0-595-19305-6

Title: New Afghanistan's TV Anchorwoman: A novel of mystery set in the New Afghanistan
ISBN: 0-595-21557-2

Title: Tools for Mystery Writers: Writing Suspense Using Hidden Personality Traits
ISBN: 0-595-21747-8

Title: The Khazars Will Rise Again!: Mystery Tales of the Khazars
ISBN: 0-595-21830-X

Title: Murder in the Women's Studies Department: A Professor Sleuth Novel of Mystery
ISBN: 0-595-21859-8

Title: Make Money With Your Camcorder and PC: 25+ Businesses: Make Money With Your Camcorder and Your Personal Computer by Linking Them.
ISBN: 0-595-21864-4

Title: Writing What People Buy: 101+ Projects That Get Results
ISBN: 0-595-21936-5

Title: Anne Joan Levine, Private Eye: Internal adventure through first-person mystery writer's diary novels
ISBN: 0-595-21860-1

Title: Verbal Intercourse: A Darkly Humorous Novel of Interpersonal Couples and Family Communication
ISBN: 0-595-21946-2

Title: The Date Who Unleashed Hell: If You Love Me, Why Do You Humiliate Me? "The Date" Mystery Fiction Series
ISBN: 0-595-21982-9

Title: Cleopatra's Daughter: Global Intercourse
ISBN: 0-595-22021-5

Title: Cyber Snoop Nation: The Adventures Of Littanie Webster, Sixteen-Year-Old Genius Private Eye On Internet Radio
ISBN: 0-595-22033-9

Title: Counseling Anarchists: We All Marry Our Mirrors—Someone Who Reflects How We Feel About Ourselves. Folding Inside Ourselves A Novel of Mystery
ISBN: 0-595-22054-1

Title: Sacramento Latina: When the One Universal We Have In Common Divides Us
ISBN: 0-595-22061-4

Title: Astronauts and Their Cats: At night, the space station is cat-shadow dark
ISBN: 0-595-22330-3

Title: How Two Yellow Labs Saved the Space Program: When Smart Dogs Shape Shift in Space
ISBN: 0-595-23181-0

Title: The DNA Detectives: Working Against Time
ISBN: 0-595-25339-3

Title: How to Interpret Your DNA Test Results For Family History & Ancestry: Scientists Speak Out on Genealogy Joining Genetics
ISBN: 0-595-26334-8

Title: Roman Justice: SPQR: Too Roman To Handle
ISBN: 0-595-27282-7

Title: How to Make Money Selling Facts: to Non-Traditional Markets
ISBN: 0-595-27842-6

Title: Tracing Your Jewish DNA For Family History & Ancestry: Merging a Mosaic of Communities
ISBN: 0-595-28127-3

Title: The Beginner's Guide to Interpreting Ethnic DNA Origins for Family History: How Ashkenazi, Sephardi, Mizrahi & Europeans Are Related to Everyone Else
ISBN: 0-595-28306-3

Title: Nutritional Genomics—A Consumer's Guide to How Your Genes and Ancestry Respond to Food: Tailoring What You Eat to Your DNA
ISBN: 0-595-29067-1

Title: How to Safely Tailor Your Food, Medicines, & Cosmetics to Your Genes: A Consumer's Guide to Genetic Testing Kits from Ancestry to Nourishment
ISBN: 0-595-29403-0

Title: One Day Some Schlemiel Will Marry Me, Pay the Bills, and Hug Me.: Parents & Children Kvetch on Arab & Jewish Intermarriage
ISBN: 0-595-29826-5

Title: Find Your Personal Adam And Eve: Make DNA-Driven Genealogy Time Capsules
ISBN: 0-595-30633-0

Title: Creative Genealogy Projects: Writing Salable Life Stories
ISBN: 0-595-31305-1

Title: Winning Resumes for Computer Personnel (Publisher: Barron's Educational Series, Inc.)
ISBN: 0-7641-0130-7

Title: Cyberscribes.1 The New Journalists (writing for the digital media)
ISBN: 1-880663-65-1

Title: Is Radical Liberalism or Extreme Conservatism a Character Disorder, Mental Disease, or Publicity Campaign?

ISBN: 0-595-31751-0

About the Author

Anne Hart, M.A., author of 43+ paperback novels and how-to books, has taken graduate work in Middle East Area Studies. Her latest book is titled ***How to Interpret Family History & Ancestry DNA Test Results for Beginners.*** Browse her books at: www.iuniverse.com. View her free instructional videos at http://www.newswriting.net.

Index

0-595-31811-8